Papa

Gordon Charles Emery

Family Genealogies of the following families:

Emery family from Windsor, Canada with roots back to France

Nathaniel Foote from England settling in Wethersfield, Connecticut

Jeremiah Donovan from County Cork, Ireland

John H. Clancy from Ireland

By Karen Emery Dwyer

Author's Notes

1. There are no living people mentioned in this book except for my immediate family from who I have permission.

2. Very often, a name, especially in the census records, would be misspelled. It was spelled as it was pronounced.   You will see in this book various spellings of the same name as I spelled the name the way I found it in the research record. Example: Foote and Foot.

3. Siblings and descendants often spelled their last names differently than their parents for many different reasons. In most cases, this was done to Americanize their name.

4. Ancestors that are in bold print are my direct line.

5. The photos on the cover of the book are of my grandparents, Mary Agnes Foote and Alcide F. Emery.

ISBN - 1450595146

EAN-13 9781450595148

© Copyright 2010 Karen Emery Dwyer
6226 Willet Court
Lakewood Ranch, Florida 34202
karensdwyer@yahoo.com

Cover by the author

Printed in the United States of America by CreateSpace, a DBA of On-Demand Publishing LLC, part of the Amazon group of companies.

Acknowledgements

Thank you to my many cousins who shared names and dates of their family's births, marriages, deaths and most of all pictures. Thankfully we were able to find each other and share our information.

A special thanks to my mother, Gertrude Bowman Emery Weyneth, who thought she was no help at all, but was a wealth of information. She was able to point me in the right direction and help me so much in piecing together the family tree. This family research has been very gratifying to me and has allowed me to meet many cousins that I never knew I had.

Karen Emery Dwyer
2010

A Word about the
Genealogical Number System

The numbering system used in this book is the Simple Register Report format, the format accepted by the New England Historic Genealogical Society, one of the oldest genealogical societies in the country. The format dates back to 1870 and is used to establish "pedigrees".

This book consists of four chapters of Genealogical Summaries. Numbers are assigned to the people covered in the genealogy.

The progenitor is given the number 1. Each child is then numbered in order with lower-case Roman numerals (i, ii, iii, iv, v, etc.) and those whose lines are carried on are also given an Arabic number. For instance, No. 1 may have had seven children (i through vii), but only one of these had descendants, say iv. No. iv is then also given the Arabic number 2 and his children, in turn, are numbered from i on, with, perhaps, Nos. i, iv and vi given the additional identification of 3, 4 and 5.

For example, in Chapter Three:

3. Mary Etta Clancy[2] (John H. Clancy[1]) was born on August 09, 1864 in Redfield, New York and died on July 11, 1923 at 1210 Churchill Avenue, Utica, New York.

Mary Etta Clancy and George L. Foote Jr had the following children:

13.   **i.**   **Mary Agnes Foote** was born August 16, 1890 in Utica, New York and died March 27, 1982 in Lakeland, Florida.
14.   ii.   Isabel L. Foote was born January 08, 1894 in Milford, Massachusetts and died August 31, 1973 in New Hartford, New York
       iii.   Edna Foote was born January 11, 1897 in Utica, New York and died September 22, 1987 in Lakeland, Florida

The bold numbers are Mary Etta and Mary Agnes' unique Arabic numbers in the system. John H. Clancy[1] with unique number [1] is the progenitor who immigrated to America. The numbers **13** and **14** for Mary Agnes and Isabel Lydia indicates they had children. Whereas Edna has the iii, which indicates she did not have children.

Table of Contents

The Relationship between the Footes, Donovan's and Clancy's

(Author's Father's Maternal Side)

The Donovan's

(Chapter Four)

The Clancy's

(Chapter Three)

Jeremiah Donovan's Daughter:

Mary Ann............... Married............... John H. Clancy

The Footes

(Chapter Two)

Their daughter   George L. Foote, Sr.'s Son

Mary Etta Clancy …..........Married…………. George L. Foote, Jr.

The relationships between the Emery's and how they connect to the Footes, Donovan's and Clancy's.

(Author's Father's Paternal Side)

The Emery's

(Chapter One)

John Baptist Emery's son
↓
Alcide Emery………… married……

The Foote's

(Chapter Two)

George L. Foote, Jr.'s daughter
↓
Mary Agnes Foote

The Emery's settled in Utica, New York.

Utica was first settled by Europeans in 1773, on the site of Fort Schuyler which was built in 1758 and abandoned after the French and Indian War. The settlement eventually became known as Old Fort Schuyler when a military fort in nearby Fort Stanwix was renamed Fort Schuyler during the American Revolution, and gradually evolved into a village. The perhaps apocryphal account of Utica's naming suggests that around a dozen citizens of the Old Fort Schuyler settlement met at the Bagg's Tavern to discuss the name of the emerging village. Unable to settle on one particular name, the name Utica was drawn from several suggestions, and the village thereafter became associated with Utica, Tunisia, the ancient Carthaginian city. [1]

Post card of the Busy Corner, Utica, New York, ca 1890 to 1900 in the personal collection of the author.

---

[1] http://en.wikipedia.org/wiki/Utica,_New_York

The <u>Foote Family</u> settled in Madison, New York

Madison was set off from Hamilton on February 6, 1807, and is one of five towns erected in the year following the formation of the county. It lies on the east border of the county south of the center and corresponds with No. 3 of the Twenty Townships. Its surface consists chiefly of a rolling upland, with intervening valleys along the course of a branch of the Chenango River and a branch of Oriskany Creek, which are the principal streams; the former flows south and the latter north. The town is abundantly watered with small brooks and springs. There are several small ponds, the principal body of water now being the Madison Brook Reservoir, in the south part, which covers 235 acres, and was connected with the Chenango Canal by a feeder. The Utica, Clinton and Binghamton Railroad runs diagonally across the town from northeast to southwest closely following the line of the abandoned Chenango Canal, and has stations at Solsville and Bouckville. According to the census of 1892 the town has a population of 2,251.[2]

This Photo of the Madison Hotel was taken in 1916. This hotel was the Foot Hotel in 1874 as indicated in Chapter Two, the Foote Family. This photo was obtained from Diane VanSlyke, Historian of Madison, New York, and used with permission.

---

[2] History of Madison, New York
FROM OUR COUNTY AND ITS PEOPLE
A DESCRIPTIVE AND BIOGRAPHICAL RECORD OF
MADISON COUNTY, NEW YORK
EDITED BY: JOHN E. SMITH
THE BOSTON HISTORY COMPANY, PUBLISHERS 1899

The <u>Clancy Family</u> settled in Redfield, New York.

Though now one of the minor towns of Oswego County in population and business, the history of Redfield goes back into the past century, and on its territory was once one of the most flourishing early settlements. Its formation as a town took place on the 14th of March, 1800, when it was taken from the great town of Mexico, then a part of Oneida County, and was the second town in chronological order formed in what later became Oswego County. It is situated in the northeastern corner of the county and a considerable portion of it is still covered by the original forest. Hilly in the southern part, its surface spreads out in the northern part, a high rolling plateau. Salmon River runs nearly east and west across the southern part, and a branch extends northward across the town in that direction, giving excellent drainage. Along this stream extends a wide intervale, the soil of which is a deep sandy loam; elsewhere the underlying rock is limestone and the soil above it is generally thin and fairly fertile. The town received the name of Redfield, in honor of Mr. Frederick Redfield, who bought a large tract of land here in early years. [3]

Photo of Main Street, Redfield, New York from Liz Grant, Historian for Redfield, New York and used with permission.

Photo of the Ben Lewis House in Redfield, New York from Liz Grant, Historian for Redfield, New York and used with permission.

---

[3] History of Redfield, NY from Landmarks of Oswego Count

The Donovan Family settled in Osceola, New York

Settlement of the town of Osceola, New York began around 1838 and was formed from the Town of West Turin in 1844. The south town line is the border of Oneida County, and the west town line is the border of Oswego County. The Salmon River flows across the south part of the town. [4]

Postcard from the collection of Larry J. Myers and used with permission.

---

[4] http://en.wikipedia.org/wiki/Osceola,_New_York#History

The Donovan Family settled in Osceola, New York but attended St. Mary's Catholic Church in Florence, New York.

Florence was formed from the Town of Camden in 1805 and was named after the city Florence in Italy[5]. The town borders Oswego County on the west and Lewis County on the north and is northwest of Rome. Florence was first settled by emigrants from Connecticut about 1798 and 1800. The Irish emigrants started coming about 1830. It now has some fine dairy farms to boast of. The town has had the name of having long winters and deep snows. The land by being devoted to the use of dairying is constantly growing better from year to year. Success, we say, to the sober, virtuous, intelligent, and working me of Florence. "An honest man is truly the noblest work of God."[6]

This postcard of Florence, New York was from the collection of Barbara Paufue and is used with permission.

---

[5] http://en.wikipedia.org/wiki/Florence,_New_York
[6] Excerpts from Rome Citizen Newspaper, Rome, New York, Wednesday, July 17, 1850

Chapter One

Descendants of
Emery Dit Coderre

Generation One

1. Emery Dit Coderre[1] was born in 1588 in France[1]. He married Andrea Jones.

Emery Dit Coderre and Andrea Jones had the following child:
      2.   **i. Magny Aymeric Emery** was born about 1620[2] and died April 13, 1674 in Sarrazac, Perigueux, Dordogne, France[3].

Generation Two

2. Magny Aymeric Emery[2] (Emery Dit Coderre[1]) was born about 1620 in Sarrazac, Perigueux, Dordogne, France and died on April 13, 1674 in Sarrazac, Perigueux, Dordogne, France[4]. He married Marguerite Pasquau on August 06, 1643 in Perigueux, Dordogne, Aquitaine, France[5]. She was born about 1620 in Sarrazac, Perigueux, Dordogne, France and died on December 06, 1687 in Sarrazac, Perigueux, Dordogne, France[6].

Magny Aymeric Emery and Marguerite Pasquau had the following child:

3.   **i.**   **Antoine Emery Dit Coderre** was born August 06, 1643 in Sarrazac, Perigueux, Limousin, France[7] and died February 10, 1716 in Contrecoeur, Vercheres, Quebec, Canada[8].

---

[1] Ancestry.com One World Tree
[2] Ancestry.com One World Tree
[3] Ancestry.com One World Tree
[4] Ancestry.com One World Tree
[5] Ancestry.com One World Tree
[6] Ancestry.com One World Tree
[7] Book: French Families of the Detroit River Region by Rev. Christian Dennisen
[8] Book: French Families of the Detroit River Region by Rev. Christian Dennisen

Generation Three

3. Antoine Emery Dit Coderre[3] (Magny Aymeric Emery[2], Emery Dit Coderre[1]) was born on August 06, 1643 in Sarrazac, Perigueux, Limousin, France[9] and died on February 10, 1716 in Contrecoeur, Vercheres, Quebec, Canada[10]. He married Marie Devault on April 16, 1674 in Contrecoeur, Vercheres, Quebec, Canada, the daughter of Jacques Devault and Louise Folure. She was born about 1649 in Nogent Le Roy (beauce), Orleanais, France[11] and died on December 06, 1687 in Repentigny, Quebec, Canada[12]. After the death of Marie Devault, Antoine married Marie Anne Favreau on June 05, 1688 in Contrecoeur, Quebec, Contract Moreau, Canada. She was the daughter of Pierre Favreau dit Deslauriers and Marie Benoint. She was born about 1672 in Contrecoeur, Vercheres, Quebec, Canada[13] and died on April 03, 1737 in Contrecoeur, Vercheres, Quebec, Canada[14].

Antoine arrived in Canada on August 17, 1665, aboard the LaPaix as a soldier in the Regiment de Carignan, company of Contrecoeur. Following two years of service, he was demobilized in 1668 and decided to remain in Canada. On April 13, 1674, Antoine and Marie Devault consented to their marriage contract in Contrecoeur, Vercheres, Quebec in the presence of notary Adhemar. There were eleven children born of this marriage, six of whom survived to adulthood. Marie Devault died on December 6, 1687 and was buried the next day at Repentigny at the same time as her last daughter who was six weeks old.

On June 5, 1688, in Boucherville, in the presence of notary Moreau, the 44 year old Antoine remarried. His new bride was Marie-Anne Favreau, the 16 year old daughter of Pierre Favreau dit Deslauries and Marie Benoit. Antoine and Pierre were both members of the same company in the Carignan Regiment. Antoine and Marie-Anne had nine children, all of whom reached adulthood. After the death of Antoine, Marie-Anne married a second time to Joseph Circe dit Saint-Michael. With Antoine the father of 15 children who had families of their own, he left a strong foundation for the growth of the Emery name in Canada.

---

[9] Book: French Families of the Detroit River Region by Rev. Christian Dennisen
[10] Book: French Families of the Detroit River Region by Rev. Christian Dennisen
[11] Book: French Families of the Detroit River Region by Rev. Christian Dennisen
[12] Book: French Families of the Detroit River Region by Rev. Christian Dennisen
[13] Book: French Families of the Detroit River Region by Rev. Christian Dennisen
[14] Ancestry.com One World Tree

Antoine Emery Dit Coderre and Marie Anne Favreau had the following child:

4.   i.   Joseph Emery Dit Coderre was born February 24, 1698 in Ste Famille, Boucherville, Quebec, Canada[15] and died April 22, 1762 in Bout De L'ile, Montreal, Quebec, Canada[16]. He married Marie Perrein, July 16, 1725 in Bout De L'ile, Montreal, Quebec, Canada.

Generation Four

4. Joseph Emery Dit Coderre[4] (Antoine Emery Dit Coderre[3], Magny Aymeric Emery[2], Emery Dit Coderre[1]) was born on February 24, 1698 in Ste Famille, Boucherville, Quebec, Canada[17] and died on April 22, 1762 in Bout De L'ile, Montreal, Quebec, Canada[18]. He married Marie Perrein on July 16, 1725 in Bout De L'ile, Montreal, Quebec, Canada. She was born on January 20, 1702 in Montreal, Quebec, Canada[19]. After the death of Marie Perrein, Joseph married Marie Louise Brunet Dit Bourbonnais on April 30, 1737 in Bout De L'ile, Montreal, Quebec, Canada. She was born on November 04, 1717 in Lachine, Quebec, Canada[20] and died on March 16, 1773 in Montreal, Quebec, Canada[21].

Joseph Emery Dit Coderre and Marie Louise Brunet Dit Bourbonnais had the following child:

5.   i.   Joseph Emery Dit Coderre was born September 11, 1744 in Bout de L'Isle, Quebec, Canada[22] and April 05, 1784 in Bout de L'Isle, Quebec, Canada[23].

---

[15] Ancestry.com One World Tree
[16] Book: French Families of the Detroit River Region by Rev. Christian Dennisen
[17] Ancestry.com One World Tree
[18] Book: French Families of the Detroit River Region by Rev. Christian Dennisen
[19] Book: French Families of the Detroit River Region by Rev. Christian Dennisen
[20] Book: French Families of the Detroit River Region by Rev. Christian Dennisen
[21] Ancestry.com One World Tree
[22] Ancestry.com One World Tree
[23] Ancestry.com One World Tree

Generation Five

5. Joseph Emery Dit Coderre[5] (Joseph Emery Dit Coderre[4], Antoine Emery Dit Coderre[3], Magny Aymeric Emery[2], Emery Dit Coderre[1]) was born on September 11, 1744 in Bout de L'Isle, Quebec, Canada[24] and died on April 05, 1784 in Bout de L'Isle, Quebec, Canada[25]. He married Marie Jeanne Parant on January 16, 1774 in St. Michel Vaudreuil, Quebec, Canada. She was born on May 29, 1753 in Lachine, Quebec, Canada[26].

Joseph Emery Dit Coderre and Marie Jeanne Parant had the following children:
  i.   Marie Louise Emery was born Pierre Labadie, January 07, 1800.
6.   ii.   **Luc Emery Dit St. Luc** was born on January 11, 1775 in Oka, Quebec, Canada[27] and died September 07, 1853 in Grande Pointe, Ontario, Canada[28].

Generation Six

6. Luc Emery Dit St. Luc[6] (Joseph Emery Dit Coderre[5] Joseph Emery Dit Coderre[4], Antoine Emery Dit Coderre[3], Magny Aymeric Emery[2], Emery Dit Coderre[1]) was born on January 11, 1775 in Oka, Quebec, Canada[29] and died on September 07, 1853 in Grande Pointe, Ontario, Canada[30]. He married Charlotte Tiriac Dit Laforest on February 04, 1805 in St. Joachim De Chateauguay, Quebec, Canada. She died on November 05, 1846 in Grande Pointe, Ontario, Canada[31].

Luc left Chateauguay, Quebec about 1811 by Bateau, because of the War of 1812; he had to stay in York (Toronto) until 1815, that same year he arrived where today is Grande

---

[24] Ancestry.com One World Tree
[25] Ancestry.com One World Tree
[26] Book: French Families of the Detroit River Region by Rev. Christian Dennisen
[27] Book: French Families of the Detroit River Region by Rev. Christian Dennisen
[28] Book: French Families of the Detroit River Region by Rev. Christian Dennisen
[29] Book: French Families of the Detroit River Region by Rev. Christian Dennisen
[30] Book: French Families of the Detroit River Region by Rev. Christian Dennisen
[31] Book: French Families of the Detroit River Region by Rev. Christian Dennisen

Pointe in Kent County, Ontario. On March 5, 1829 Luc applied and was granted land: Lot 7, Concession 8, Dover East Twp in Kent County, Ontario.

Luc Emery Dit St. Luc and Charlotte Tiriac Dit Laforest had the following children:

       i.   Charlotte Emery was born September 30, 1805 in Chateauguay, Quebec, Canada[32] and died June 19, 1886 in Grande Pointe, On, Canada[33]. She married Joseph Maillet on February 04, 1823 in St. Pierre River Thames.

7.   ii.   **Luc Emery Dit Coderre** was born about 1807 in Chateauguay, Quebec, Canada[34] and died January 12, 1885 in Grande Pointe, Ontario, Canada[35].

     iii.   Emerence Emery was born about 1807 in Chateauguay, Quebec, Canada[36] and died June 25, 1854 in Grande Pointe, Ontario, Canada[37]. She married Pierre Raymond Dit Toulouse on February 06, 1826 in St. Pierre River Thames.

     iv.   Rosalie Emery was born September 11, 1808 in Chateauguay, Quebec, Canada[38]. She married Simon Drouillard on August 01, 1825 in St. Pierre River Thames.

     v.   Alexis Emery was born September 09, 1810 in Chateauguay, Quebec, Canada[39]. She married Francoise Pelletier, April 26, 1836 in St. Pierre River Thames.

     vi.   Marie Emery was born January 16, 1812 in Chateauguay, Quebec, Canada[40] and died November 13, 1855 in Grande Pointe, On, Canada[41]. She married Raymond Dit Toulouse, February 12, 1828 in St. Pierre River Thames.

     vii.   Suzanne Emery was born February 27, 1813 in York, Upper Canada[42]. She married Olivier Hebert, May 24, 1829 in St. Pierre River Thames.

    viii.   Victoire Emery was born February 17, 1815 in York, Upper Canada[43]. She married Daniel Hathaway, October 22, 1832 in St. Pierre River Thames[44].

     ix.   Genevieve Emery was born August 12, 1817 in Grande Pointe, Ontario, Canada[45]. She married Benjamin Charron, May 14, 1839 in St. Pierre River Thames.

     x.   Joseph Emery was born October 05, 1819 in Grande Pointe, Ontario, Canada[46]. He married Felicite Faubert, February 20, 1843 in St. Pierre River Thames.

[32] Book: French Families of the Detroit River Region by Rev. Christian Dennisen
[33] Book: French Families of the Detroit River Region by Rev. Christian Dennisen
[34] Book: French Families of the Detroit River Region by Rev. Christian Dennisen
[35] Book: French Families of the Detroit River Region by Rev. Christian Dennisen
[36] Book: French Families of the Detroit River Region by Rev. Christian Dennisen
[37] Book: French Families of the Detroit River Region by Rev. Christian Dennisen
[38] Book: French Families of the Detroit River Region by Rev. Christian Dennisen
[39] Book: French Families of the Detroit River Region by Rev. Christian Dennisen
[40] Book: French Families of the Detroit River Region by Rev. Christian Dennisen
[41] Book: French Families of the Detroit River Region by Rev. Christian Dennisen
[42] Book: French Families of the Detroit River Region by Rev. Christian Dennisen
[43] Book: French Families of the Detroit River Region by Rev. Christian Dennisen
[44] Book: French Families of the Detroit River Region by Rev. Christian Dennisen
[45] Book: French Families of the Detroit River Region by Rev. Christian Dennisen
[46] Book: French Families of the Detroit River Region by Rev. Christian Dennisen

xi.   Francois Emery Dit Coderre was born November 27, 1822 in Grande Pointe, Ontario, Canada[47] and died May 23, 1895 in Grande Pointe, Ontario, Canada[48]. He married Josephte Alexandre, November 06, 1843 in St. Pierre River Thames.

Generation Seven

7. Luc Emery Dit Coderre[7] (Luc Emery Dit St. Luc[6], Joseph Emery Dit Coderre[5] Joseph Emery Dit Coderre[4], Antoine Emery Dit Coderre[3], Magny Aymeric Emery[2], Emery Dit Coderre[1]) was born about 1807 in Chateauguay, Quebec, Canada[49]. He died on January 12, 1885 in Grande Pointe, Ontario, Canada[50]. He married Charlotte Hebert in 1828 in St. Pierre River Thames. She was born in 1810 in Quebec [51] died on July 07, 1874 in Grande Pointe, Ontario, Canada[52].

Luc Emery Dit Coderre and Charlotte Hebert had the following children:
    i.   Charlotte Emery was born October 04, 1829 in Grande Pointe, Ontario, Canada[53] and died September 01, 1830 in Grande Pointe, On, Canada[54].
    ii.   Marie Emery was born May 30, 1831 in Grande Pointe, Ontario, Canada, and died February 13, 1855 in Grande Pointe, Ontario, Canada. She married Antoine Labadie, August 24, 1852 in St. Pierre River Thames.
    iii.   Luc Emery was born about 1833 and died August 10, 1848 in Grande Pointe, Ontario, Canada.
    iv.   Alexandre Emery was born October 25, 1834 in Grande Pointe, Ontario Canada[55] and died February 17, 1873 in Paincourt, Ontario, Canada[56]. He married Catherine Rheaume February 09, 1858 in Immaculate Conception De Paincourt, Ontario, Canada.
    v.   Charles Emery was born October 29, 1836 in St. Pierre In Tilbury E. Ontario, Canada[57], and died December 15, 1894 in Grande Pointe, Ontario, Canada[58]. He

---

[47] Book: French Families of the Detroit River Region by Rev. Christian Dennisen
[48] Book: French Families of the Detroit River Region by Rev. Christian Dennisen
[49] Book: French Families of the Detroit River Region by Rev. Christian Dennisen
[50] Book: French Families of the Detroit River Region by Rev. Christian Dennisen
[51] Quebec Vital Records Vital and Church Records (Drouin Collection) 1621 to 1967 at Ancestry.com
[52] Book: French Families of the Detroit River Region by Rev. Christian Dennisen
[53] Book: French Families of the Detroit River Region by Rev. Christian Dennisen
[54] Book: French Families of the Detroit River Region by Rev. Christian Dennisen
[55] Book: French Families of the Detroit River Region by Rev. Christian Dennisen
[56] Church Records – deaths Immaculate Conception, PainCourt, Ontario, Canada
[57] Church Records – deaths St. Philippe, Grand Pointe, Ontario, Canada
[58] Church Records – deaths St. Philippe, Grand Pointe, Ontario, Canada

married Catherine Primeau, May 29, 1860 in Immaculate Conception De Paincourt, Ontario, Canada.

8.   vi.   Francois-Luc Emery was born September 21, 1838[59] and died July 10, 1912 in Grande Pointe, Ontario, Canada[60].

vii.   Joseph Emery was born May 02, 1840 in Grande Pointe, Ontario, Canada[61] and died November 03, 1840 in Grande Pointe, Ontario, Canada[62].

9.   viii.   Jean (John) Baptist Emery Dit Coderre was born September 05, 1841 in Grande Pointe, Ontario, Canada[63] and died August 31, 1904 in New York Mills, Oneida County, New York[64].

ix.   Joseph Emery was born August 29, 1843 in Grande Pointe, Ontario, Canada[65] and died October 25, 1931 in Listowel, Ontario, Canada[66]. He married Julie Lecuyer, February 25, 1868 in Immaculate Conception De Paincourt, Ontario, Canada.

x.   Helene Emery was born March 13, 1845 in Grande Pointe, Ontario, Canada[67] and died August 22, 1876 in Grande Pointe, Ontario, Canada[68]. She married William Thibodeau, June 23, 1863 in Immaculate Conception De Paincourt, Ontario, Canada.

xi.   Adele Emery was born April 28, 1847 in Grande Pointe, Ontario, Canada[69]. She married Alexandre Foster, April 30, 1874 in Immaculate Conception De Paincourt, Ontario, Canada.

xii.   Felice Emery was born January 01, 1849[70]. She married Janvier Frederic Lussier, May 20, 1873 in Immaculate Conception De Paincourt, Ontario, Canada.

xiii.   Jacques (James) Emery was born August 18, 1850 in St Joseph Chatam, Ontario, Canada and died September 26, 1908 in Grande Pointe, Ontario, Canada[71]. He married Henriette Faubert, January 25, 1870 in Immaculate Conception De Paincourt, Ontario, Canada.

10.   xiv.   Antoine Emery was born April 07, 1852 in Grande Pointe, Ontario, Canada[72] and died April 17, 1936 in Chatham, Ontario, Canada[73].

---

[59] Church Records – deaths St. Philippe, Grand Pointe, Ontario, Canada
[60] Church Records – deaths St. Philippe, Grand Pointe, Ontario, Canada
[61] Book: French Families of the Detroit River Region by Rev. Christian Dennisen
[62] Book: French Families of the Detroit River Region by Rev. Christian Dennisen
[63] Book: French Families of the Detroit River Region by Rev. Christian Dennisen
[64] Death Certificate from Whitestown, New York
[65] Church Records – deaths Immaculate Conception, PainCourt, Ontario, Canada
[66] Book: French Families of the Detroit River Region by Rev. Christian Dennisen
[67] Church Records – deaths Immaculate Conception, PainCourt, Ontario, Canada
[68] Church Records – deaths Immaculate Conception, PainCourt, Ontario, Canada
[69] Church Records – deaths Immaculate Conception, PainCourt, Ontario, Canada
[70] Church Records – deaths Immaculate Conception, PainCourt, Ontario, Canada
[71] Church Records – deaths St. Philippe, Grande Pointe, Ontario, Canada and French families of the Detroit River Region
[72] Church Records – deaths Immaculate Conception, PainCourt, Ontario, Canada
[73] Book: French Families of the Detroit River Region by Rev. Christian Dennisen

xv.   Edesse Emery was born April 07, 1852 in Grande Pointe, Ontario, Canada[74] and died March 09, 1932 in Grande Pointe, Ontario, Canada[75]. She married David Houle, January 21, 1884 in Immaculate Conception De Paincourt, Ontario, Canada. Edesse was a twin to Antoine.

xvi.   Elizabeth Jeanne (Betsy) Emery was born May 09, 1854 in Grande Pointe, Ontario, Canada[76]. She married Andre Richer, November 06, 1884 in Immaculate Conception De Paincourt, Ontario, Canada.

Generation Eight

8. Francois-Luc Emery[8] (Luc Emery Dit Coderre[7], Luc Emery Dit St. Luc[6], Joseph Emery Dit Coderre[5] Joseph Emery Dit Coderre[4], Antoine Emery Dit Coderre[3], Magny Aymeric Emery[2], Emery Dit Coderre[1]1) was born on September 21, 1838[77] and died on July 10, 1912 in Grande Pointe, Ontario, Canada[78]. He married Rosalie Tetreault on September 10, 1861 in Immaculate Conception De Paincourt, Ontario, Canada. She was born on August 23, 1841 in St Jean, Quebec, Canada[79] and died on July 29, 1927 in Grande Pointe, Ontario, Canada.

Francois-Luc Emery and Rosalie Tetreault had the following children:

i.   Cyrille Emery was born June 03, 1862 in Grande Pointe, Ontario, Canada[80] and died March 23, 1863 in Grande Pointe, Ontario, Canada[81].

ii.   Narcisse Emery was born July 19, 1863 in Grande Pointe, Ontario, Canada[82] and died in Windsor, Ontario, Canada[83].

iii.   Lisa Emery was born January 19, 1865 in Grande Pointe, Ontario, Canada[84] and died in Seattle, Washington.

iv.   Remi Salomon Emery was born December 30, 1866 in Grande Pointe, Ontario, Canada and died May 01, 1924 in Grande Pointe, Ontario, Canada[85].

---

[74] Church Records – deaths St. Philippe, Grande Pointe, Ontario, Canada and French families of the Detroit River Region
[75] Book: French Families of the Detroit River Region by Rev. Christian Dennisen
[76] Church Records – deaths St. Philippe, Grande Pointe, Ontario, Canada and French families of the Detroit River Region
[77] Church Records – deaths St. Philippe, Grande Pointe, Ontario, Canada
[78] Church Records – deaths St. Philippe, Grande Pointe, Ontario, Canada
[79] Church Records – Marriages Immaculate Conception, PainCourt, Ontario, Canada
[80] Book: French Families of the Detroit River Region by Rev. Christian Dennisen
[81] Book: French Families of the Detroit River Region by Rev. Christian Dennisen
[82] Book: French Families of the Detroit River Region by Rev. Christian Dennisen
[83] Book: French Families of the Detroit River Region by Rev. Christian Dennisen
[84] Book: French Families of the Detroit River Region by Rev. Christian Dennisen
[85] Book: French Families of the Detroit River Region by Rev. Christian Dennisen

v.   Marie Malvina Emery was born January 10, 1869 in Grande Pointe, Ontario, Canada[86] and died in Montana[87].

vi.   Rose Delima Emery was born August 05, 1870 in Grande Pointe, Ontario, Canada[88] and died April 19, 1875 in Grande Pointe, Ontario, Canada[89].

vii.   Alfred David Emery was born May 22, 1873 in Grande Pointe, Ontario, Canada and died January 20, 1932 in Paincourt, Ontario, Canada.   Alfred was ordained to priesthood by Bishop McEvay.

viii.   Francois Xavier Emery was born February 17, 1875 in Grande Pointe, Ontario, Canada[90] and died in Grande Pointe, Ontario, Canada[91].

ix.   Pamela Marie Emery was born November 26, 1876 in Grande Pointe, Ontario, Canada[92] and died in Windsor, Ontario, Canada[93].

x.   Zephyr Emery was born August 27, 1878 in Grande Pointe, Ontario, Canada[94] and died in Windsor, Ontario, Canada[95].

xi.   Louis Alcide Emery was born September 23, 1880 in Grande Pointe, Ontario, Canada[96] and died in Saginaw, Michigan[97].

xii.   Amedee Felix Emery was born June 26, 1882 in Grande Pointe, Ontario, Canada[98] and died April 25, 1902 in Grande Pointe, Ontario, Canada[99].

xiii.   Female Emery was born June 08, 1886 in Grande Pointe, Ontario, Canada[100] and died June 08, 1886 in Grande Pointe, Ontario, Canada[101].

xiv.   Joseph Arsene Herve Emery was born January 31, 1889 in Grande Pointe, Ontario, Canada[102] and died September 17, 1931 in Paincourt, Ontario, Canada[103].

9.   Jean (John) Baptist Emery Dit Coderre[8] (Luc Emery Dit Coderre[7], Luc Emery Dit St. Luc[6], Joseph Emery Dit Coderre[5] Joseph Emery Dit Coderre[4], Antoine Emery Dit Coderre[3], Magny Aymeric Emery[2], Emery Dit Coderre[1]1) was born on September 05, 1841 in Grande Pointe, Ontario, Canada[104] and died on August 31, 1904 in New York

[86] Book: French Families of the Detroit River Region by Rev. Christian Dennisen
[87] Book: French Families of the Detroit River Region by Rev. Christian Dennisen
[88] Book: French Families of the Detroit River Region by Rev. Christian Dennisen
[89] Book: French Families of the Detroit River Region by Rev. Christian Dennisen
[90] Book: French Families of the Detroit River Region by Rev. Christian Dennisen
[91] Book: French Families of the Detroit River Region by Rev. Christian Dennisen
[92] Book: French Families of the Detroit River Region by Rev. Christian Dennisen
[93] Book: French Families of the Detroit River Region by Rev. Christian Dennisen
[94] Book: French Families of the Detroit River Region by Rev. Christian Dennisen
[95] Book: French Families of the Detroit River Region by Rev. Christian Dennisen
[96] Book: French Families of the Detroit River Region by Rev. Christian Dennisen
[97] Book: French Families of the Detroit River Region by Rev. Christian Dennisen
[98] Book: French Families of the Detroit River Region by Rev. Christian Dennisen
[99] Book: French Families of the Detroit River Region by Rev. Christian Dennisen
[100] Book: French Families of the Detroit River Region by Rev. Christian Dennisen
[101] Book: French Families of the Detroit River Region by Rev. Christian Dennisen
[102] Book: French Families of the Detroit River Region by Rev. Christian Dennisen
[103] Book: French Families of the Detroit River Region by Rev. Christian Dennisen
[104] Book: French Families of the Detroit River Region by Rev. Christian Dennisen

Mills, Oneida County, New York[105]. Jean was baptized in October 1841 in St. Pierre, Ontario, Canada[106]. He married Philomene Tetreault on May 13, 1862 in Grande Pointe, Ontario, Canada. She was the daughter of Narcisse Tetreault and Archange Remillard. She was born on June 03, 1843 in St. Jean, Quebec, Canada[107] and died on February 28, 1880 in Paincourt, Ontario, Canada[108]. After the death of Philomene he married Celina Gagnier on June 05, 1883 in Essex, Ontario, Canada[109]. She was born on February 10, 1858 in Montreal, Quebec, Canada[110] and died on April 20, 1944 in 18 Ellis Avenue, Whitesboro, Oneida County, New York[111].

The History of the Emery Family
by Ella Cushman in 1986

John Baptiste Emery and his family traveled from Windsor, Canada to North Adams, Massachusetts in 1900. About a year later they moved from North Adams to New York Mills, New York where their youngest son, Louis was born. They lived on Main Street across from the post office. When they left Canada, they had been living on a farm that they owned on the shores of Lake St. Claire. The youngest son from John's first marriage bought the farm from his father.

Death notice only - September 1, 1904 - Utica Daily Press

John Emery died at his home in this village of New York Mills at 10 o'clock this morning. He was a native of Canada and was 62 years old.

John had married twice having ten children in his first marriage. His first wife died bearing twins who also died at the same time. His second wife had twelve children. Three of these children died at a young age.

Jean (John) Baptist Emery Dit Coderre and Philomene Tetreault had the following children:
      i.   Marie Rosena Emery was born in 1863[112] and died in 1869 in St. Paul, Joliette, Quebec[113].

---

[105] Death Certificate
[106] Ontario, Canada, Catholic Church Records (Drouin Collection), 1747-1967 at Ancestry.com
[107] Book: French Families of the Detroit River Region by Rev. Christian Dennisen
[108] Book: French Families of the Detroit River Region by Rev. Christian Dennisen
[109] Ontario, Canada Marriages, 1801-1926 at Ancestry.com
[110] Death Certificate
[111] Death Certificate
[112] Church Records – Marriages Immaculate Conception, PainCourt, Ontario, Canada
[113] Quebec Vital and Church Records (Drouin Collection) 1621 to 1967 at Ancestry.com

ii.   David Jean Emery was born October 10, 1865[114] and died September 19, 1869 in Paincourt, Ontario, Canada[115].

iii.   Nellie Emery was born about 1867 in Ontario, Canada. She married a man by the name of Tiebedeau. She joined St Joseph's convent in Winnipeg after her husband disappeared one day at the train station. She had two girls who died young.

iv.   Adelaide Emery was born February 28, 1867[116] and died June 06, 1868 in Paincourt, Ontario, Canada[117].

11.   v.   Cesarie Emery was born 1868[118].

12.   vi.   Ambrose Emery was born in 1874[119] and died February 23, 1939[120].

13.   vii.   Jean-Baptiste Emery was born about 1878 in Ontario, Canada.

14.   viii.   Lucy Emery was born about 1878[121] in St. Joachim, Ontario, Canada and died September 10, 1898[122] in St. Joachim, Ontario, Canada

ix.   Adelaide Emery was born October 1878[123] and died December 31, 1880 in Ontario, Canada[124].

x.   Anonyme (Un-Named Child) Emery was born in 1880 and died February 02, 1880[125].

---

[114] Church Records – deaths Immaculate Conception, PainCourt, Ontario, Canada
[115] Church Records – deaths Immaculate Conception, PainCourt, Ontario, Canada
[116] Church Records – deaths Immaculate Conception, PainCourt, Ontario, Canada
[117] Church Records – deaths Immaculate Conception, PainCourt, Ontario, Canada
[118] Church Records – Marriages Immaculate Conception, PainCourt, Ontario, Canada
[119] Church Records – deaths Immaculate Conception, PainCourt, Ontario, Canada
[120] Church Records – deaths Immaculate Conception, PainCourt, Ontario, Canada
[121] Ontario Death Records
[122] Ontario Death Records
[123] Ontario Death Records
[124] Ontario Death Records
[125] Church Records – deaths Immaculate Conception, PainCourt, Ontario, Canada

Obituary - Utica Daily Press - April 21, 1944

Whitesboro - Mrs. Celina Emery, 85, died April 20, 1944, in her home, 18 Ellis Ave. after a lingering illness. Born in Canada February 10, 1859, she was married to John Emery. He died in 1904. Mrs. Emery had lived here for a number of years and was a member of St. Paul's Church. She leaves five sons, Fred, Utica; Wilfred and Otis, Whitesboro; Leo, Detroit, and Louis, Clinton; four daughters, Mrs. Fred Bechard, Chittenango, Mrs. George Zimmer, Yorkville; Mrs. John Brosmer, Troy, and Mrs. John Cain in California; 24 grandchildren and 23 great-grandchildren.

Photo of the Emery family taken in 1900 from the author's collection.

Celina was the oldest of 14 children. One of her sisters drowned in a well when she was 8 years old and just made her first communion.

Jean (John) Baptist Emery Dit Coderre and Celina Gagnier had the following children:

      i.   Roselima Emery was born March 20, 1884 in Stoney Point, Ontario, Canada[126] and died April 10, 1981 in Community Hospital Fontana, San Bernardino, California[127]. She married Frederick Moses Bechard in 1910 in St Paul's Catholic Whitesboro, Oneida, New York. Roselima raised a niece, Marie, but had no natural children.

Photo of Rose Emery from the collection of Richard Emery and used with permission.

---

[126] Obituary Utica Newspaper, April 11, 1981
[127] Obituary Utica Newspaper, April 11, 1981

Obituary - Utica Observer Dispatch - April 12, 1981
Whitesboro - Mrs. Roselima Bechard, 97, of Fontana, Calif. and formerly of Whitesboro, died April 10, 1981 in Community Hospital, San Bernadino, Calif. She was born in Ontario, Canada, March 21, 1884, daughter of John and Celina Gagnier Emery and came to the United States in 1900. She married Fred M. Bechard in 1910 in St. Paul's Church, Whitesboro. He died in 1962. Mrs. Bechard was a member of St. Paul's Church. She is survived by one sister, Mrs. Eva Harp of Fontana; several nieces who include Mrs. W. (Marie) Hogan of Port Charlotte, Florida, and several nephews also survive. The funeral will be Wednesday morning at 9:30 at the J.W. Dimbleby Funeral Home and at 10:00 at St. Paul's Church. Interment will be in Mount Olivet Cemetery. Calling hours Tuesday 2-4 and 7-9.

15.   ii.   Alcide F. Emery was born May 18, 1885 in Stoney Point, Ontario, Canada[128] and died July 12, 1961 in Faxton Hospital Utica, New York[129].
16.   iii.   Wilfred Napoleon Emery was born November 23, 1886 in Stoney Point, Ontario, Canada[130] and died July 11, 1951 in 18 Ellis Avenue, Whitesboro, New York[131].
17.   iv.   Laura L. Emery was born January 30, 1888 in Stoney Point, Ontario, Canada[132] and died February 21, 1950 in St. Lukes Memorial Hospital, New Hartford, New York[133].
18.   v.   Alfred P. Emery was born January 14, 1890 in Stoney Point, Ontario, Canada[134] and died June 17, 1940 at 2131 Highland Avenue., Utica, New York[135].
19.   vi.   Otis A. Emery was born May 15, 1891 in St. Claire, Ontario, Canada[136] and died June 12, 1947 at 17 Brainard Street, Whitesboro, New York[137].
   vii.   Emile Emery was born April 30, 1894 in Ontario, Canada[138] and died January 31, 1908 in New York Mills, New York[139].

Obituary - Utica Daily Press - February 1, 1908

Death of Emile Emery, a Bright Popular Young Ladd. New York Mills, January 31st at the family home, No. 311 Main street, at 3 o'clock this morning, occurred the death of Emile Emery. Three months ago he contracted a severe cold, which developed into

[128] Mt. Oliviet Cemetery Records, Whitesboro, New York
[129] Obituary Utica Newspaper, July 13, 1961
[130] Obituary Utica Newspaper, July 12, 1951
[131] Obituary Utica Newspaper, July 12, 1951
[132] Canadian Birth Records
[133] Mt. Oliviet Cemetery Records, Whitesboro, New York
[134] Mt. Oliviet Cemetery Records, Whitesboro, New York
[135] Obituary Utica Newspaper, June 18, 1940
[136] Obituary Utica Newspaper, June 13, 1947
[137] Obituary Utica Newspaper, June 13, 1947
[138] Canadian Birth Records
[139] Obituary Utica Newspaper, February 1, 1908

consumption, and he failed rapidly. Emil Emery was born in Canada 13 years ago, the son of the late John and Salina Emery. When a small boy he came to this village with his parents. He attended the Middle Mills Union School and was a bright active little fellow, well liked by his school associates. He leaves six brothers and four sisters, besides his mother. The family has the sympathy of the community in their bereavement. The funeral will be held from the home at 9:30 o'clock Monday morning and a half hour later from St. Paul's Catholic Church in Whitesboro.

20.   viii.   Marie Beatrice Emery was born July 14, 1895 in Stoney Point, Ontario, Canada[140] and died October 27, 1949 in Troy, New York[141].

21.   ix.   Leo Anthony Emery was born February 23, 1897 in Stoney Point, Ontario, Canada[142] and died in 1953 in Detroit, Michigan.

22.   x.   Eva M. Emery was born November 14, 1899 in Tecumseh, Ontario, Canada[143] and died October 20, 1983 in Fontana, San Bernardino, California[144].

xi.   Agnes Emery was born before 1900 in Ontario, Canada and died soon after at age eight months in Ontario, Canada.

23.   xii.   Louis C. Emery was born October 17, 1902 in New York Mills, New York[145] and died March 27, 1959 in Clinton, New York[146].

10. Antoine Emery[8] (Luc Emery Dit Coderre[7], Luc Emery Dit St. Luc[6], Joseph Emery Dit Coderre[5] Joseph Emery Dit Coderre[4], Antoine Emery Dit Coderre[3], Magny Aymeric Emery[2], Emery Dit Coderre[1]) was born on April 07, 1852 in Grande Pointe, Ontario, Canada[147]. He died on April 17, 1936 in Chatham, Ontario, Canada[148]. He married Mathilde Lauzon on February 07, 1875 in Immaculate Conception De Paincourt, Ontario, Canada. She was born about 1853[149].

Antoine Emery and Mathilde Lauzon had the following children:

i.   Emile Emery was born January 27, 1873 in Ontario, Canada[150].

ii.   Angeline Emery was born February 18, 1887 in Ontario, Canada[151].

iii.   Bergere Emery was born September 16, 1895 in Ontario, Canada[152].

[140] Ontario, Canada Births, 1869-1909
[141] New York State Vital Records, Syracuse, New York
[142] World War I draft registration on Ancestry.com
[143] Social Security Death Index at Ancestry.com
[144] Social Security Death Index at Ancestry.com
[145] Obituary Utica Newspaper, March 28, 1959
[146] Obituary Utica Newspaper, March 28, 1959
[147] Church Records – Marriages Immaculate Conception, PainCourt, Ontario, Canada
[148] Book: French Families of the Detroit River Region by Rev. Christian Dennisen
[149] Church Records – Marriages Immaculate Conception, PainCourt, Ontario, Canada
[150] 1901 Canadian Census at Ancestry.com
[151] 1901 Canadian Census at Ancestry.com
[152] 1901 Canadian Census at Ancestry.com

iv.   Maggie Emery was born April 18, 1897 in Ontario, Canada[153].

v.   Theodore Emery was born October 22, 1883 in Canada[154].

Generation Nine

11. Cesarie Emery[9] (Jean (John) Baptist Emery Dit Coderre[8], Luc Emery Dit Coderre[7], Luc Emery Dit St. Luc[6], Joseph Emery Dit Coderre[5] Joseph Emery Dit Coderre[4], Antoine Emery Dit Coderre[3], Magny Aymeric Emery[2], Emery Dit Coderre[1]) was born in 1868[155]. She married Francis Hall on September 10, 1888.

Photo of Cesarie Emery and Francis Hall from the collection of James Miller and used with permission.

Cesarie Emery and Francis Hall had the following children:

i.   William Dennis Hall was born in 1889 in Tilbury, Kent County, Ontario, Canada[156]. He married Emma Godreau on July 25, 1910 in Scaunton, Virginia.

ii.   Rose Emma Hall was born in 1894 in Tilbury, Kent County, Ontario, Canada[157].

iii.   Mary (Minnie) Hall was born in 1895 in Tilbury, Kent County, Ontario, Canada[158].

iv.   Francis Hall was born in 1898 in Tilbury, Kent County, Ontario, Canada[159]. He married Bertha Trepanier on October 09, 1930 in Churchville, New York.

v.   Joseph Frank Hall was born in 1898 in Tilbury, Kent County, Ontario, Canada[160].

vi.   Loretta Hall was born in 1900 in Tilbury, Kent County, Ontario, Canada[161].

vii.   Alfred Hall was born 1905 in Tilbury, Kent County, Ontario, Canada[162].

[153] 1901 Canadian Census at Ancestry.com
[154] 1901 Canadian Census at Ancestry.com
[155] Canadian Birth Records
[156] Family Information from James M. Miller
[157] Family Information from James M. Miller
[158] Family Information from James M. Miller
[159] Family Information from James M. Miller
[160] Family Information from James M. Miller
[161] Family Information from James M. Miller
[162] Family Information from James M. Miller

viii.   Walter Bernabe Hall was born 1906 in Tilbury, Kent County, Ontario, Canada[163].

ix.   Victor Hall was born in 1908 in Tilbury, Kent County, Ontario, Canada[164].

24.   x.   Helen Hall was born in 1911 in Tilbury, Kent County, Ontario, Canada[165] and died in 1968[166].

12. Ambrose Emery[9] (John Baptist Emery Dit Coderre[8], Luc Emery Dit Coderre[7], Luc Emery Dit St. Luc[6], Joseph Emery Dit Coderre[5] Joseph Emery Dit Coderre[4], Antoine Emery Dit Coderre[3], Magny Aymeric Emery[2], Emery Dit Coderre[1])[49] was born in 1874[167] and died on February 23, 1939[168]. He married Clarisse Plante on October 14, 1895 in Hempstead, New York, the daughter of Olivier Plante and Emilie Dufrense. She died in 1915[169]. After the death of Clarisse, Ambrose married Charlotte Ray on October 02, 1916 in Belle River, Essex, Ontario, Canada daughter of Joseph Ray and Caroline Dauphin. She died in January 1939.

Ambrose Emery and Clarisse Plante had the following children:

i.   Marie Lilly Annie Emery was born July 24, 1898 in Merrick, New York[170]and died January 19, 1901.

25.   ii.   Leon Eluid Emery was born February 22, 1900 in Merrick, New York[171].

26.   iii.   George Wilfred Emery was born February 09, 1902[172].

iv.   Blanche Alma Emery was born May 08, 1904[173].

v.   Marie Odorina Emery was born November 03, 1905[174].

13. Jean-Baptiste Emery[9] (John Baptist Emery Dit Coderre[8], Luc Emery Dit Coderre[7], Luc Emery Dit St. Luc[6], Joseph Emery Dit Coderre[5] Joseph Emery Dit Coderre[4], Antoine Emery Dit Coderre[3], Magny Aymeric Emery[2], Emery Dit Coderre[1]) was born about 1878 in Ontario, Canada. He married Emelie Dicaire on July 14, 1902. She was the daughter of Joseph Dicaire and Emelie Chevalier. Jean purchased the family farm from his father when his father immigrated to the USA in 1900.

---

[163] Family Information from James M. Miller
[164] Family Information from James M. Miller
[165] Family Information from James M. Miller
[166] Family Information from James M. Miller
[167] Family Information from James M. Miller
[168] Family Information from James M. Miller
[169] Family Information from James M. Miller
[170] Family Information from James M. Miller
[171] Family Information from James M. Miller
[172] Family Information from James M. Miller
[173] Family Information from James M. Miller
[174] Family Information from James M. Miller

Photo of Jean-Baptiste Emery on the family farm in Canada in the collection of Richard Emery and used with permission.

Jean-Baptiste Emery and Emelie Dicaire had the following children:

       i.   Dora Lea Emery was born August 09, 1904.

14. Lucy Emery[9] (John Baptist Emery Dit Coderre[8], Luc Emery Dit Coderre[7], Luc Emery Dit St. Luc[6], Joseph Emery Dit Coderre[5] Joseph Emery Dit Coderre[4], Antoine Emery Dit Coderre[3], Magny Aymeric Emery[2], Emery Dit Coderre[1]) was born in 1878[175]. She died on September 10, 1898. She married Alexander Plante, November 13, 1894 in St. Joachim, Ontario, Canada[176]. He was the son of Olivier Plante and Emilie Dufrene.

Lucy Emery and Alexandre Plante had the following child:

       i.   Edward Plante was born in 1891. He married Ella St. Pierre on September 01, 1919.

15. **Alcide F. Emery**[9] (John Baptist Emery Dit Coderre[8], Luc Emery Dit Coderre[7], Luc Emery Dit St. Luc[6], Joseph Emery Dit Coderre[5] Joseph Emery Dit Coderre[4], Antoine Emery Dit Coderre[3], Magny Aymeric Emery[2], Emery Dit Coderre[1]) was born on May 18, 1885 in Stoney Point, Ontario, Canada[177] and died on July 12, 1961 in Faxton Hospital Utica, New York [178]. He married Mary Agnes Foote on July 14, 1909 in St. Patrick's Church, Utica, New York[179]. She was the daughter of George L. Foote and Mary Etta Clancy. She was born on August 16, 1890 in Utica, New York[180] and died on March 27, 1982 in Lakeland, Florida[181]. For more on Mary Agnes Foote, see Chapter Two.

Alcide was baptized in L'annoanciation De Pointe-aux-r, Catholic and his baptismal name - Joseph Philias Alcide.

---

[175] Family Information from James M. Miller
[176] Ontario, Canada Marriages 1857 - 1924
[177] Obituary Utica Newspaper, July 13, 1961
[178] Obituary Utica Newspaper, July 13, 1961
[179] New York State Vital Records
[180] Death Certificate
[181] Death Certificate

He came with his family to the United States on the Grand Trunk Railroad from St. Clair, Canada. At time of Naturalization, Alcide Emery lived at 1701 Erie St., Utica, New York. He became a U.S. citizen June 26, 1920 in Utica, New York, at the Oneida County Court House.

Alcide (Fred) was my grandfather. What I remember about him is that he was an usher at Sacred Heart Church. He worked at the Utica & Mohawk Cotton Mills and retired in 1952. His occupation was listed as a loom fixer, mill hand. He was also a carpenter. I remember the doll house he built for his granddaughters to play with. When my father built our house, my grandfather was there every day sweeping up and organizing the tools so my dad could start working again as soon as he finished his days work at Chicago Pneumatic. When my father would drive up and see his father's car in front of the house, he would say "there's old faithful".

Photo of Alcide Emery from the author's collection.

Obituary - Utica Daily Press July 14, 1961

Alcide (Fred) F. Emery, 76, of 1131 Downer Ave., died Wednesday in Faxton Hospital. He was born in Ontario, Canada, and came to New York Mills from Ontario when he was 21. He came to Utica in 1906, and he had since lived here. Mr. Emery was a loom fixer for the Utica & Mohawk Cotton Mills, Inc. until he retired in 1952. He married M. Agnes Foote in 1909. Mr. Emery was a member of the Church of the Sacred Heart, its Holy Name Society and Men's Club. Besides his wife, he leaves two sons, Harold, New Hartford, and Gordon, Sauquoit, two sisters, Mrs. Fred Beechern, Chittenango, and Mrs. Lynn Harp, Fontana, Calif. The funeral will be at 8:30 tomorrow from the Heintz Funeral Home, and at 9:00 from the Church of the Sacred Heart, where a solemn Requiem Mass will be offered. Burial will be in Mt. Olivet Cemetery. The Holy Name Society of the church will meet at the funeral home at 8 tonight to recite the rosary.

Alcide F. Emery and Mary Agnes Foote had the
following children:

27.   i.   Harold Alcide Emery was born July 21,
1913 in Utica, New York and died December 11, 1989
in New Hartford, New York[182].

28.   ii.   **Gordon Charles Emery** was born
March 29, 1915 in Utica, New York and died October
09, 1981 in St. Luke's Hospital, New Hartford, New
York.[183]

Photo of Mary Agnes Foote from the author's collection.

16. Wilfred Napoleon Emery[9] (John Baptist Emery Dit Coderre[8], Luc Emery Dit
Coderre[7], Luc Emery Dit St. Luc[6], Joseph Emery Dit Coderre[5] Joseph Emery Dit
Coderre[4], Antoine Emery Dit Coderre[3], Magny Aymeric Emery[2], Emery Dit Coderre[1])

was born on November 23, 1886 in Stoney Point, Ontario,
Canada[184], and died on July 11, 1951 at 18 Ellis Avenue,
Whitesboro, New York[185]. He married Lina C. Chicoine on
January 08, 1907 in St Paul's Catholic Church, Whitesboro,
New York. She was born on March 28, 1886 in Canada[186] and
died on November 03, 1984 at18 Ellis Avenue, Whitesboro,
New York[187].

*Photo of Wilfred Napoleon Emery from the collection of Richard
Emery and used with permission.*

---

[182] Obituary Utica Newspaper, December 12, 1989
[183] Death Certificate
[184] Obituary Utica Newspaper, July 12, 1951
[185] Obituary Utica Newspaper, July 12, 1951
[186] Obituary Utica Newspaper, November 4, 1984
[187] Obituary Utica Newspaper, November 4, 1984

Obituary - Utica Daily Press - July 12, 1951

Whitesboro - Wilfred N. (Bill) Emery, 65, of 18 Ellis Avenue, died July 11, 1951, in his home after a five month illness. He was born November 23, 1886, in Stony Point, Ontario, Canada, a son of John and Celina Gagnier Emery. He married Lina Chicoine January 8, 1907, in St. Paul's Church, Whitesboro. He was a communicant of St. Paul's Church and a member of its Holy Name Society. He was employed as a loom fixer at the Mohawk Cotton Mill. He came to this country and New York Mills in 1900 and had lived in Whitesboro for the past 26 years. Besides his wife, he leaves six daughters, Mrs. Ella Cushman, Waterville, Mrs. George Heller, Rome; Mrs. William Hall, Sauquoit; Mrs. Armand Ramaccia, Whitesboro; Mrs. Thomas Cunningham and Mrs. Donald Grahame, both of Utica; five sons, Frederick E., Oriskany; Clifford J., Whitesboro; Charles H., Waterville; Wilfred L., Wisconsin; and Harry Emery, Utica; two sisters, Mrs. Fred Bechard, Chittenango; Mrs. James Cain, California; three brothers, Alcide, Utica; Leo, Detroit; Louis Emery, Clinton; and 29 grandchildren.   The funeral will be at 8:45 Saturday from the Langdon Funeral Home, York and Maple, and at 9:30 from St. Paul's Church where a Solemn Requiem High Mass will be celebrated. Burial will be in Mt. Olivet Cemetery.

Wilfred Napoleon Emery and Lina C. Chicoine had the following children:

29.   i.   Ella Anna Emery was born March 15, 1908 in New York Mills, New York[188] and died March 19, 2006 in Utica, New York[189].

30.   ii.   Frederick E. Emery was born January 20, 1910 on Main Street, Yorkville, New York, and died November 03, 1973 in St. Luke's Memorial Hospital, New Hartford, New York[190].

31.   iii.   Loretta Emery was born June 13, 1911 in New York Mills, New York, and died March 21, 1974 in Sarasota, Florida[191].

32.   iv.   Irene Celina Emery was born January 04, 1913 in New York Mills, New York, and died January 14, 1977 in Faxton Hospital, Utica, New York[192].

33.   v.   Blanche Edna Emery was born March 05, 1914 in New York Mills, New York, and died May 19, 1993 in St. Luke's Hospital, New Hartford, New York[193].

34.   vi.   Clifford J. Emery was born December 05, 1916 in New York Mills, New York[194] and died March 16, 1996 in Ellis Hospital Schenectady, New York[195].

---

[188] Obituary Utica Newspaper, March 20, 2006
[189] Obituary Utica Newspaper, March 20, 2006
[190] Obituary Utica Newspaper, November 4, 1973
[191] Obituary Utica Newspaper, March 22, 1974
[192] Obituary Utica Newspaper, January 15, 1977
[193] Obituary Utica Newspaper, May 20, 1993
[194] Obituary Utica Newspaper, March 17, 1996
[195] Obituary Utica Newspaper, March 17, 1996

35.   vii.   Marion Emery was born May 27, 1918 in Yorkville, New York, and died November 16, 1995 in Albany Medical Center, Albany, New York[196].

36.   viii.   Charles Henry Emery was born December 14, 1919 in Yorkville, New York[197], and died October 23, 2001 in Waterville, New York[198].

37.   ix.   Wilfred L. Emery was born October 21, 1923 in New York Mills, New York, and died December 03, 2005 in Milwaukee, Wisconsin[199].

       x.   Living Emery

      xi.   Living Emery

Photo of the family of Wilfred and Lina Emery from the collection of Beverly Gargas and used with permission. First Row: Harry, Lina, Wilfred, Harriet. Second Row: Marion, Fred, Blanche, Charles, Ella, Clifford, Loretta, Wilfred, and Irene.

17. Laura L. Emery[9] (Jean (John) Baptist Emery Dit Coderre[8], Luc Emery Dit Coderre[7], Luc Emery Dit St. Luc[6], Joseph Emery Dit Coderre[5] Joseph Emery Dit Coderre[4], Antoine Emery Dit Coderre[3], Magny Aymeric Emery[2], Emery Dit Coderre[1]) was born on January 30, 1888 in Stoney Point, Ontario, Canada[200], and died on February 21, 1950 in St. Lukes Memorial Hospital, New Hartford, New York[201]. She married George R. Zimmer in August 1919 in St. Patrick's Church, Utica, New York, the son of John B. Zimmer and Dorothea Gehinig. He was born on May 19, 1890 in New York State[202] and died on June

[196] Obituary Utica Newspaper, November 17, 1995

[197] Obituary Utica Newspaper, October 24, 2001

[198] Obituary Utica Newspaper, October 24, 2001

[199] Obituary Utica Newspaper, December 4, 2005

[200] Canadian Birth Records

[201] Obituary Utica Newspaper, February 22, 1950

[202] Social Security Death Index at Ancestry.com

29, 1979 in St. Luke's Hospital, New Hartford, New York[203]. Laura's birth records gave the name of Lawrence Emery, a female.

Obituary - Utica Daily Press - February 22, 1950
Mrs. George R. Zimmer, 62, of 925 Inman Pl., died February 21, 1950 in St. Luke's Hospital after an illness of two months. Laura I. Emery was born in Stony Point, Canada January 30, 1888. She had lived most of her life in New York Mills and Yorkville. She was married to Mr. Zimmer in St. Patrick's Church in August 1919. For many years she had been a member of Sacred Heart Church. Mrs. Zimmer was a member of the Mother's Club of the Church, the Altar Society and the Women's Club. She was a member of the American Legion Auxiliary of Whitestown Post 1113. Surviving are her husband, one daughter, Mrs. Russell Joy, Nevada; one son, Raymond Zimmer, Yorkville; four brothers, William Emery, Whitesboro, Alcide, Utica; Louis, Clinton, and Leo Emery,

Detroit; and two sisters, Mrs. Fred Bechard, Chittenango, and Mrs. James Cain, Oregon. The funeral will be from the S. Roy Fisher Funeral Home, 417 Court, at 9 a.m. Friday and at 9:30 from Sacred Heart Church. Burial will be in Mount Olivet Cemetery, Whitesboro. She is buried in block 4, tier 2, grave 7&8. Interment # 3310.

Laura's baptism record gives name as Irene Laurentia. She lived at 925 Inman Place, Utica, New York when she died. George R. Zimmer attended Utica Schools and worked for Whitesboro Central School.

Photo of Laura Emery from the collection of Richard Emery and used with permission.

Laura L. Emery and George R. Zimmer had the following children:
38.   i.   Raymond George Zimmer was born February 29, 1924 in Utica, New York[204], and died May 21, 2009, at Community General Hospital, Syracuse New York[205].
        ii.   Living Zimmer

Photo of George R. Zimmer from the collection of Richard Emery and used with permission.

---

[203] Social Security Death Index at Ancestry.com
[204] Obituary, Syracuse Post Standard, May 22, 2009
[205] Obituary, Syracuse Post Standard, May 22, 2009

18. Alfred P. Emery[9] (Jean (John) Baptist Emery Dit Coderre[8], Luc Emery Dit Coderre[7], Luc Emery Dit St. Luc[6], Joseph Emery Dit Coderre[5] Joseph Emery Dit Coderre[4], Antoine

Emery Dit Coderre[3], Magny Aymeric Emery[2], Emery Dit Coderre[1]) was born on January 14, 1890 in Stoney Point, Ontario, Canada[206] and died on June 17, 1940 at 2131 Highland Avenue, Utica, New York[207]. He married Mary Ellen DuBois Kennedy on January 08, 1913 in St. Francis deSales Church, Utica, New York[208], the daughter of Richard Kennedy and Josephine DuBois. She was born on June 22, 1887 in Utica, New York[209], and died on November 14, 1953 in Memorial Hospital, Utica, New York[210]. Alfred's birth record gave the name of Philippe Dolphis Emery.

Photo of Alfred P. Emery from the collection of Richard Emery and used with permission.

Obituary - Utica Daily Press - June 18, 1940

Alfred P. Emery - The funeral services for Alfred P. Emery, 50, 2131 Highland Avenue, who died unexpectedly from an attack of heart disease Monday, June 17, 1940, will be held at 9 a.m. Thursday from his home and at 9:30 from the Church of the Sacred Heart. Mr. Emery died in his home one day after he had complained of a heart ailment. Dr. Gordon A. Holden, coroner, said death was due to that illness. Mr. Emery was born in St. Clair, Canada, son of Mrs. Celina and the late John Emery. He came to New York mills when a boy and was educated in the public schools of this vicinity. Most of his life had been spent in Utica, where he was a member of the Church of the Sacred Heart and the Holy Name Society. He married Mary DuBois, Jan. 8, 1927, who survives. Mr. Emery had been employed as a filer at the Savage Arms Corporation. Besides his mother and wife, he leaves three children, Mrs. John Ladd, Miss Winifred Emery and John Emery, all of Utica; five brothers, Fred, Utica; Wilfred and Otis Emery, Whitesboro; Leo, Detroit, and Louis Emery, Utica; four sisters, Mrs. Rose Bechard and Mrs. Louis Zimmer, both of Utica; Mrs. John Brosmer, Albany; and Mrs. James Kane, Pasadena, California.

---

[206] Obituary Utica Newspaper, June 18, 1940
[207] Obituary Utica Newspaper, June 18, 1940
[208] Obituary Utica Newspaper, June 18, 1940
[209] Obituary Utica Newspaper, November 15, 1953
[210] Obituary Utica Newspaper, November 15, 1953

Photo of Alfred P. Emery, Mary Ellen DuBois Kennedy, Beatrice Emery and the brother of Mary Ellen from the collection of Richard Emery and used with permission.

Mary died of cancer. She had been employed for 30 years by the Sturges Manufacturing Company. She was a member of the Church of the Sacred Heart and its Alter Society.

Alfred P Emery and Mary Ellen DuBois Kennedy had the following children:

39.   i.   Doris Josephine Emery was born September 20, 1916 in Utica, New York[211], and died September 08, 2006 in Folts Home, Herkimer, New York[212].

40.   ii.   Winifred M. Emery was born December 21, 1919 in Utica, New York, and died February 10, 2002 in St. Lukes Memorial Hospital, New Hartford, New York[213].

41.   iii.   John "Jack" D. Emery was born January 27, 1923 in Utica, New York, and died July 20, 2003 in New York Mills, New York[214].

19. Otis A. Emery[9] (Jean (John) Baptist Emery Dit Coderre[8], Luc Emery Dit Coderre[7], Luc Emery Dit St. Luc[6], Joseph Emery Dit Coderre[5] Joseph Emery Dit Coderre[4], Antoine Emery Dit Coderre[3], Magny Aymeric Emery[2], Emery Dit Coderre[1]) was born on May 15, 1891 in St. Claire, Ontario, Canada[215], and died on June 12, 1947 at 17 Brainard Street, Whitesboro, New York[216]. He married Mary A. Mullen on August 16, 1911 in St Paul's Catholic Church, Whitesboro, New York[217]. She was born in October 14, 1885[218] in Cohoes, New York and died on September 13, 1970 in 1045 Azusa Avenue West, Covina, California[219]. Otis was born Ozias according to his birth record.

---

[211] Obituary Utica Newspaper, September 9, 2006
[212] Obituary Utica Newspaper, September 9, 2006
[213] Social Security Death Index at Ancestry.com
[214] Obituary Utica Newspaper, July 21, 2003
[215] Obituary Utica Newspaper, June 13, 1947
[216] Obituary Utica Newspaper, June 13, 1947
[217] Wedding Announcement, Utica Newspaper
[218] California Death Index at Ancestry.com
[219] Obituary Utica Newspaper, September 24, 1970

Photo of Otis A. Emery from the collection of Richard Emery and used with permission.

Obituary - Utica Daily Press - June 13, 1947

Otis Emery, 56, 17 Brainard, Whitesboro, died June 12, 1947 in his home after an illness of six months. Born May 25, 1891 at St. Claire, Canada, he was the son of the late John and Salina Gaynor. The family came to the United States in 1900 and settled in Massachusetts but later moved to New York Mills. He was educated in New York Mills schools. August 16, 1911, Mr. Emery married Mary A. Mullen in St. Paul's Church, Whitesboro. He was a loom fixer all of his life and was so employed by the Utica Mohawk & Steam Cotton Mills until his illness. He was a member of St. Paul's Church and it's Holy Name Society, also the Maccabees. Survivors are his wife; two sons, Walter, Utica and Thomas, Whitesboro; two daughters, Mrs. George Schoen, Whitesboro, and Mrs. Paul Ensworth, Los Angeles; four brothers, A. Fred, Utica; William, Whitesboro; Leo, Detroit, and Louis, Clinton; four sisters, Mrs. Fred Beechard, Chittenango; Mrs. George Zimmer, Utica; Mrs. John Bosmer, Troy and Mrs. James Kane, Santa Monica, California; and four grandchildren. The funeral will be Monday morning from the residence and from St. Paul's Church, Whitesboro. A solemn requiem high Mass will be celebrated. Burial will be in Mt. Olivet Cemetery, Whitesboro.

Otis A. Emery and Mary A Mullen had the following children:

42.   i.   Walter Sylvester Emery was born April 24, 1912 in Whitesboro, New York[220] and died March 07, 1984 in St. Elizabeth Hospital Utica, New York[221].

43.   ii.   Genevieve Emery was born April 24, 1912 in Whitesboro, New York and died March 3, 2003 in Orleans, Massachusetts.[222]

44.   iii.   Thomas Joseph Emery was born June 24, 1913 in Whitesboro, New York[223] and died October 31, 1958 in St Luke's Hospital, Utica, New York[224].

---

[220] Obituary Utica Newspaper, March 8, 1984
[221] Obituary Utica Newspaper, March 8, 1984
[222] Family information from Dick Emery
[223] Obituary Utica Newspaper, November 1, 1958
[224] Obituary Utica Newspaper, November 1, 1958

45.   iv.   Irene Veronica Emery was born August 22, 1915 in Whitesboro, New York and died December 03, 1989 in Los Angeles, California[225].

Photo of Otis A. Emery and his wife Mary A. Mullen from the collection of Richard Emery and used with permission.

20. Marie Beatrice Emery[9] (Jean (John) Baptist Emery Dit Coderre[8], Luc Emery Dit Coderre[7], Luc Emery Dit St. Luc[6], Joseph Emery Dit Coderre[5] Joseph Emery Dit Coderre[4], Antoine Emery Dit Coderre[3], Magny Aymeric Emery[2], Emery Dit Coderre[1]) was born on July 14, 1895 in Stoney Point, Ontario, Canada[226] and died on October 27, 1949 in Troy, New York[227]. She married Roy Clark about April 1919[228]. She later married John Frederick Brosemer. John was born April 18, 1899 and died July 1965 in Averill Park, New York[229].

Photo of Beatrice Emery from the collection of Richard Emery and used with permission.

Marie Beatrice Emery and Roy Clark had the following child:
    i.   Marguerite Clark.

Photo of Beatrice Emery with her husband, Roy Clark, and her daughter, Marguerite from the collection of Richard Emery and used with permission.

---

[225] California Death Index at Ancestry.com
[226] Canadian Birth Records
[227] New York State Vital Records, Syracuse, New York
[228] Marriage License Announcement, Utica Newspaper
[229] Social Security Death Index at Ancestry.com

21. Leo Anthony Emery[9] (Jean (John) Baptist Emery Dit Coderre[8], Luc Emery Dit Coderre[7], Luc Emery Dit St. Luc[6], Joseph Emery Dit Coderre[5] Joseph Emery Dit Coderre[4], Antoine Emery Dit Coderre[3], Magny Aymeric Emery[2], Emery Dit Coderre[1]) was born on February 23, 1897 in Stoney Point, Ontario, Canada[230], and died in 1953 in Detroit, Michigan. He married Mildred J. Sharpe on April 29, 1918[231]. She was born in 1898 in New York State[232]. Leo lived at 1527 Lincoln Avenue on June 5, 1918 at the time of his draft registration. The 1920 and 1930 Detroit Census indicated he lived with his wife in Detroit, Michigan.

Leo Anthony Emery and Mildred J. Sharpe had the following children:

46.   i.   Lorraine Emery was born August 25, 1919 in Michigan[233] and died June 29, 2002 in Mesa, Arizona[234].

   ii.   Leo Anthony Emery Jr. was born April 23, 1923 in Michigan[235] and died in 1988[236]. Leo was married twice. He had two boys by his first wife. His second wife had a boy and a girl. Leo died at age 65 and is buried in Florida. His wife and children still live in Florida. The boys have children, but I do not know how many.

Photo of Leo Emery, George Zimmer, Laura Emery Zimmer and Mildred J. Shape Emery from the collection of Richard Emery and used with permission.

22. Eva M. Emery[9] (Jean (John) Baptist Emery Dit Coderre[8], Luc Emery Dit Coderre[7], Luc Emery Dit St. Luc[6], Joseph Emery Dit Coderre[5] Joseph Emery Dit Coderre[4], Antoine Emery Dit Coderre[3], Magny Aymeric Emery[2], Emery Dit Coderre[1]) was born on November 14, 1899 in Tecumseh, Ontario, Canada[237], and died on October 20, 1983 in Fontana, San Bernardino, California[238]. She married James J. Cain on August 1, 1921 at St. Patrick's Church, Utica, New York[239]. He was born in 1895 in New York State. She married Lynn C. Harp before 1961 in California. He was born on August 03, 1898[240],

---

[230] World War I draft registration on Ancestry.com
[231] Wedding Announcement, Utica Newspaper
[232] 1930 Detroit, Michigan Census
[233] Social Security Death Index at Ancestry.com
[234] Social Security Death Index at Ancestry.com
[235] Family information from Lorraine Benedict
[236] Family information from Lorraine Benedict
[237] Social Security Death Index at Ancestry.com
[238] Social Security Death Index at Ancestry.com
[239] Wedding Announcement, Utica Newspaper
[240] Social Security Death Index at Ancestry.com

and died on October 11, 1972 in Fontana, San Bernardino, California[241].   She lived in Macomb, Michigan, in the 1930 census.

Eva M. Emery and James J. Cain had the following children:

      i.   James J. Cain Jr. was born 1924 in New York State[242]. He died in an automobile accident.

      ii.   Marion Cain was born 1923 in New York State[243].

Photo of Eva M. Emery from the collection of Richard Emery and used with permission.

23. Louis C. Emery[9] (Jean (John) Baptist Emery Dit Coderre[8], Luc Emery Dit Coderre[7], Luc Emery Dit St. Luc[6], Joseph Emery Dit Coderre[5] Joseph Emery Dit Coderre[4], Antoine Emery Dit Coderre[3], Magny Aymeric Emery[2], Emery Dit Coderre[1]) was born on October 17, 1902 in New York Mills, New York[244] and died on March 27, 1959 in Clinton, New York[245].   He married Mary LeClair on September 13, 1927. She was born in 1900 in Chateaugay, New York[246] and died on March 01, 1962 in Faxton Hospital, Utica, New York[247].

Obituary - Utica Daily Press - March 27, 1959

Clinton - Louis C. Emery, 56, of 138 Utica Road, died unexpectedly March 27, 1959. in his home. Death was caused by a heart attack. Mr. Emery had been employed by the Utica Transit Corporation and its predecessor, the New York State Railways for 39 years, first as a street car conductor and later a bus driver. He was born October 17, 1902, in New York Mills, a son of John and Celina Gagnier Emery. He attended St. Joseph's School, Utica. His marriage to Mary LeClair of Churubusco, Clinton County, took place September 13, 1927. They had been residents of Clinton for the past 18 years. Mr. Emery was a member of St. Mary's Church, this village, and its Holy Name Society. Besides his wife, he leaves a daughter, Mrs. Wayne Gaffney, Chadwicks; two sisters, Mrs. Fred Beechard, Chittenango, and Mrs. Lynn Harp, Fontana, Calif.; a brother, Fred,

---

[241] Social Security Death Index at Ancestry.com
[242] 1930 Michigan Census
[243] 1930 Michigan Census
[244] Obituary Utica Newspaper, March 28, 1959
[245] Obituary Utica Newspaper, March 28, 1959
[246] Obituary Utica Newspaper, March 2, 1962
[247] Obituary Utica Newspaper, March 2, 1962

Utica and several nieces and nephews. The funeral will be at 9 Monday from the Owens Funeral Home and at 9:30 from St. Mary's church where a solemn Requiem High Mass will be offered.

Mary was a member of St. Mary's Church in Clinton, New York, its Altar and Rosary Society, the Women's Club and Clinton Grange. Louis C. Emery and Mary LeClair had one child who may still be living.

Generation Ten

24. Helen Hall[10] (Cesarie Emery[9], Jean (John) Baptist Emery Dit Coderre[8], Luc Emery Dit Coderre[7], Luc Emery Dit St. Luc[6], Joseph Emery Dit Coderre[5] Joseph Emery Dit Coderre[4], Antoine Emery Dit Coderre[3], Magny Aymeric Emery[2], Emery Dit Coderre[1]) was born in 1911 in Tilbury, Kent County, Ontario, Canada[248] and died in 1968[249]. She married Cyprein Caron. He was born in 1901 and died in 1989[250]. Helen Hall and Cyprein Caron had three children who may still be living.

Photo of Helen Hall and Cyprein Caron on their wedding day from the collection of James Miller and used with permission.

25. Leon Eluid Emery[10] (Ambrose Emery[9], John Baptist Emery Dit Coderre[8], Luc Emery Dit Coderre[7], Luc Emery Dit St. Luc[6], Joseph Emery Dit Coderre[5] Joseph Emery Dit Coderre[4], Antoine Emery Dit Coderre[3], Magny Aymeric Emery[2], Emery Dit Coderre[1]) was born on February 22, 1900 in Merrick, New York [251]. He married Francoise Beaulieu on October 12, 1925, the daughter of Alexandre Beaulieu and Agnes Brooker.

Leon Eluid Emery and Francoise Beaulieu had the following children:
      i.   Joseph Eliud Marc Emery was born August 04, 1926 in Lewis County General Hospital, Lowville, New York [252] and died August 06, 1926.

---

[248] Family Information from James M. Miller
[249] Family Information from James M. Miller
[250] Family Information from James M. Miller
[251] Family Information from James M. Miller
[252] Family Information from James M. Miller

    ii.   Living Emery
    iii.   Living Emery
    iv.   Living Emery

26. George Wilfred Emery[10] (Ambrose Emery[9], John Baptist Emery Dit Coderre[8], Luc Emery Dit Coderre[7], Luc Emery Dit St. Luc[6], Joseph Emery Dit Coderre[5] Joseph Emery Dit Coderre[4], Antoine Emery Dit Coderre[3], Magny Aymeric Emery[2], Emery Dit Coderre[1]) was born on February 09, 1902[253]. He married Eva Chouinard on October 01, 1923, the daughter of Narcisse Chouinard and Alma Trudeau. He later married Marie Rheaume on January 14, 1977, the daughter of Charles Rheaume and Petronille (Elizabeth) Tremblay. She was born on June 11, 1905 in Germany[254].

George Wilfred Emery and Eva Chouinard had the following children:
    i.   Jean-Paul Emery was born in 1923[255] and died May 16, 1930[256].
    ii.   Living Emery
    iii.   Living Emery
    iv.   Jeanette Gertrude Emery was born in 1929 and died March 21, 1962 in Hempstead, New York[257]. She married James Strong, June 09, 1951.
    v.   Living Emery
    vi.   Living Emery
    vii. Living Emery

---

[253] Family Information from James M. Miller
[254] Family Information from James M. Miller
[255] Family Information from James M. Miller
[256] Family Information from James M. Miller
[257] Family Information from James M. Miller

27. Harold Alcide Emery[10] (Alcide F Emery[9], Jean (John) Baptist Emery Dit Coderre[8], Luc Emery Dit Coderre[7], Luc Emery Dit St. Luc[6], Joseph Emery Dit Coderre[5] Joseph Emery Dit Coderre[4], Antoine Emery Dit Coderre[3], Magny Aymeric Emery[2], Emery Dit Coderre[1]) was born on July 21, 1913 in Utica, New York[258] and died on December 11, 1989 in New Hartford, New York[259]. He married Marie Longtin on January 08, 1938 in Utica, New York, the daughter of Paul and Amelia Longtin. She was born on January 29, 1916[260] in Norristown, Pennsylvania and died on January 01, 1990 in New Hartford, New York[261].

Photo of Harold Alcide Emery from the author's collection.

Harold was a graduate of Utica Free Academy and The Philadelphia College of Pharmacy and Science. He was the founder of Emery Pharmacy on the corner of James and Neilson Streets in Utica, New York. He served his country as a Lieutenant in the U.S. Navy during World War II. He and his wife were members of St. John the Evangelist Church in New Hartford, New York. Harold was past president of the Mohawk Valley Pharmaceutical Society and a member of the American Society of Consultant Pharmacists, the Utica Elks Lodge #31 and honorary life member of the William E. Burke Utica Council #189 Knights of Columbus. Harold Alcide Emery and Marie Longtin had two children who are still living.

28. Gordon Charles Emery[10] (Alcide F Emery[9], Jean (John) Baptist Emery Dit Coderre[8], Luc Emery Dit Coderre[7], Luc Emery Dit St. Luc[6], Joseph Emery Dit Coderre[5] Joseph Emery Dit Coderre[4], Antoine Emery Dit Coderre[3], Magny Aymeric Emery[2], Emery Dit Coderre[1]) was born on March 29, 1915 in Utica, New York[262] and died on October 09, 1981 in St. Luke's Hospital, New Hartford, New York[263]. He married Gertrude Marie Bowman on April 26, 1941 in St. Joseph's Church, Utica, New York, thedaughter of George Francis Bowman and Susanna Etta Sifer[264]. She was born on January 14, 1920 in Utica, New York. Gordon was a World War II Navy Veteran and worked for many years as a lab technician at Chicago Pneumatic Tool Company retiring in 1973.

[258] Obituary Utica Newspaper, December 12, 1989

[259] Obituary Utica Newspaper, December 12, 1989

[260] Obituary Utica Newspaper, January 1, 1990

[261] Obituary Utica Newspaper, January 1, 1990

[262] Death Certificate

[263] Death Certificate

[264] Marriage Certificate

He was past president and honorary member of the Sauquoit Valley Rotary Club. Gordon and Gertrude retired in 1973 and purchased a travel trailer. They drove to Arizona twice to spend the winter. They took in many sites along the way. They both treasured those years, but after a few years they settled in Bradenton, Florida for the winters.

Gordon Charles Emery and Gertrude Marie Bowman had the following children:

  i.   **Karen Susanne Emery** married Martin Jay Dwyer in 1968 and has one daughter, two grandsons and two step grandsons.

  ii.   Gaile Joyce Emery married Michael John Shimon in 1979 and has one daughter and one grandson.

Photo of Gordon Charles Emery and Gertrude Marie Bowman on their wedding day, April 26, 1941, from the author's collection.

29. Ella Anna Emery[10] (Wilfred Napoleon Emery[9], Jean (John) Baptist Emery Dit Coderre[8], Luc Emery Dit Coderre[7], Luc Emery Dit St. Luc[6], Joseph Emery Dit Coderre[5] Joseph Emery Dit Coderre[4], Antoine Emery Dit Coderre[3], Magny Aymeric Emery[2], Emery Dit Coderre[1]) was born on March 15, 1908 in New York Mills, New York[265] and died on March 19, 2006 in Utica, New York[266]. She married Leroy W. Cushman on September 23, 1931 in St. Paul's Church, Whitesboro, New York[267], the son of Frederick Francis Cushman and Mary Retersdorf. He was born on March 04, 1901 in Marcy, New York and died on October 01, 1946 in Memorial Hospital, Utica, New York[268]. At an early age Ella went to Canada with her parents but returned to the United States when she entered first grade. She could only speak French when she returned and always praised her wonderful first grade teacher. The teacher stayed after school every day helping her until she could speak English. Ella in turn went home and taught her mother English. Ella loved school but had to quit school to help the family financially. She returned to night school many years later to earn her GED. She worked as a seamstress for Marcy State Hospital for many years. She was a life-long member of St. Paul's Catholic Church in Whitesboro, New York.

[265] Obituary Utica Newspaper, March 20, 2006
[266] Obituary Utica Newspaper, March 20, 2006
[267] Obituary Utica Newspaper, March 20, 2006
[268] Obituary Utica Newspaper, October 2, 1946

Leroy lived in Whitesboro most of his life where for ten years he was employed as a cabinet maker by the Quigley Furniture Company and eight years by the Marcy State Hospital. He had operated a farm near Waterville for the two years prior to his death. He was a member of St. Bernard's Church in Waterville, New York.

Ella Anna Emery and Leroy W. Cushman had the following children:

     i.   Richard Cushman was born March 25, 1933 and died June 02, 1933.

     ii.   Ronald E. Cushman was born June 20, 1936 and April 30, 1999 in Stittville, New York[269].

     iii.   Living Cushman

Photo of Ella Anna Emery from the collection of Richard Emery and used with permission.

30. Frederick E. Emery[10] (Wilfred Napoleon Emery[9], Jean (John) Baptist Emery Dit Coderre[8], Luc Emery Dit Coderre[7], Luc Emery Dit St. Luc[6], Joseph Emery Dit Coderre[5] Joseph Emery Dit Coderre[4], Antoine Emery Dit Coderre[3], Magny Aymeric Emery[2], Emery Dit Coderre[1]) was born on January 20, 1910 in Main Street, Yorkville, New York and died on November 03, 1973 in St. Luke's Memorial Hospital, New Hartford, New York[270]. He married Margaret T. Smith on September 29, 1933 in St. Stephen's Church, Oriskany, New York[271], the daughter of Louis Smith and Freda Schmidt. She was born on February 22, 1913 and died December 27, 1994 in Oriskany, New York.[272] Frederick attended New York Mills and Whitesboro Schools. Prior to his employment at Ibbotson's, he worked for Harry Heiman, Carbon Motors and Geffen Motors. He was a member of St. Stephen's Church, its Holy Name Society and the Usher's Club. Margaret was educated in Oriskany schools. Margaret was a seamstress at the Eastern Star Home. She also made rosaries for others as a member of the Rosary Makers Guild. Frederick E. Emery and Margaret T. Smith had six children who still may be living.

---

[269] Obituary Utica Newspaper, May 1, 1999
[270] Obituary Utica Newspaper, November 4, 1973
[271] Obituary Utica Newspaper, November 4, 1973
[272] Social Security Death Index at Ancestry.com

31. Loretta Emery[10] (Wilfred Napoleon Emery[9], Jean (John) Baptist Emery Dit Coderre[8], Luc Emery Dit Coderre[7], Luc Emery Dit St. Luc[6], Joseph Emery Dit Coderre[5] Joseph Emery Dit Coderre[4], Antoine Emery Dit Coderre[3], Magny Aymeric Emery[2], Emery Dit Coderre[1]) was born on June 13, 1911 in New York Mills, New York and died on March 21, 1974 in Sarasota, Florida[273]. She married George Frederick Heller on February 28, 1932 in Marcy, New York, the son of George F. Heller Sr. and Josephine Maloney. He was born on March 18, 1911 in Utica, New York and died on October 23, 1984 in Rome, New York[274]. After her marriage, Loretta lived in Utica and Canajoharie before moving to Rome in 1944. She was a member of St. Peter's Church.

Loretta Emery and George Frederick Heller had the following children:
  i.   Living Heller
  ii.   Living Heller
  iii. Living Heller
  iv.   Living Heller
  v.   Diane Joan Heller was born August 07, 1940 in Utica, New York and died March 14, 1979. She was married on September 27, 1958 in Rome, New York.

32. Irene Celina Emery[10] (Wilfred Napoleon Emery[9], Jean (John) Baptist Emery Dit Coderre[8], Luc Emery Dit Coderre[7], Luc Emery Dit St. Luc[6], Joseph Emery Dit Coderre[5] Joseph Emery Dit Coderre[4], Antoine Emery Dit Coderre[3], Magny Aymeric Emery[2], Emery Dit Coderre[1]) was born on January 04, 1913 in New York Mills, New York and died on January 14, 1977 in Faxton Hospital, Utica, New York[275]. She married William Hall on January 04, 1936 in St. Paul's Church, Whitesboro, New York, the son of William Hall Sr. and Elizabeth O'Neill. He was born on May 25, 1909 in Utica, New York and died on November 28, 1984. Irene was born in New York Mills and attended school there. Irene had retired from General Electric receiver works in 1973 and was a member of St. Patrick's Church in Clayville, New York. Irene Emery and William Hall had two children who may still be living.

33. Blanche Edna Emery[10] (Wilfred Napoleon Emery[9], Jean (John) Baptist Emery Dit Coderre[8], Luc Emery Dit Coderre[7], Luc Emery Dit St. Luc[6], Joseph Emery Dit Coderre[5] Joseph Emery Dit Coderre[4], Antoine Emery Dit Coderre[3], Magny Aymeric Emery[2], Emery Dit Coderre[1]) was born on March 05, 1914[276] in New York Mills, New York and died on May 19, 1993 in St. Luke's Hospital, New Hartford, New York. She married

---

[273] Obituary Utica Newspaper, March 22, 1974
[274] Obituary Utica Newspaper, October 24, 1984
[275] Obituary Utica Newspaper, January 15, 1977
[276] Obituary Utica Newspaper, May 20, 1993

Thomas James Cunningham on June 15, 1935 in Utica, New York, the son of Claude J. Cunningham and Agnes Dobbins.[277] He was born on March 22, 1914 in Utica, New York[278] and died on August 23, 1988.[279] Blanche had been employed for several years at the Horrocks Ibbotson Company and later the Mele Manufacturing Co. She was a member of St. Peter's Church, North Utica and its Altar Rosary Society. She was a member and past president of the Deerfield Senior Citizens. Thomas was employed by Horrocks Ibbotson Company for 45 years until his retirement. He was also a member of St. Peter's Church in North Utica. Blanche Edna Emery and Thomas James Cunningham had one child who may still be living

34. Clifford J. Emery[10] (Wilfred Napoleon Emery[9], Jean (John) Baptist Emery Dit Coderre[8], Luc Emery Dit Coderre[7], Luc Emery Dit St. Luc[6], Joseph Emery Dit Coderre[5] Joseph Emery Dit Coderre[4], Antoine Emery Dit Coderre[3], Magny Aymeric Emery[2], Emery Dit Coderre[1]) was born December 5, 1916 in New York Mills, New York[280] and died March 16, 1996 at Ellis Hospital, Schenectady, New York[281]. He married Stella Ann Pluta on October 23, 1941 at St. Paul's Church, Whitesboro, New York. She was the daughter of Stanley Pluta and Anna Pendrak. Clifford received his education at Whitesboro High School and Utica College. He was a World War II Veteran serving in the 96th Infantry Division and spent three years in San Diego and almost three years in the Pacific Theater, participating in the Battle of Leyete Gulf, Philippines. He was a part of the invasion force at Okinawa on Easter of 1945 and also served in the Japan Occupation Force. He was a traffic manager at International Heater of Utica from 1946 to 1983, a member of St. Paul's Church and the Utica Traffic Club. He taught public speaking at UFA Adult Education and was a graduate instructor with Dale Carnegie Courses for many years.

Clifford J. Emery and Stella Ann Pluta had the following children:
  i.   Living Emery
  ii.   Living Emery
  iii.   Donald J. Emery was born January 26, 1950 in Utica, New York[282] and died July 23, 1972 in Herkimer County, New York[283]. Donald died of a drowning accident. He was educated in St. Paul's Elementary School, Whitesboro and graduated in 1969 from Notre Dame High School. He was a student at the State University at Buffalo.

---

[277] Obituary Utica Newspaper, May 20, 1993
[278] Obituary Utica Newspaper, August 24, 1988
[279] Obituary Utica Newspaper, August 24, 1988
[280] Obituary Utica Newspaper, March 17, 1996
[281] Obituary Utica Newspaper, March 17, 1996
[282] Obituary Utica Newspaper, July 24, 1972
[283] Obituary Utica Newspaper, July 24, 1972

He was a member of St. Paul's Church, Whitesboro, and in his earlier years served as an altar boy. He was also a member of the Notre Dame High tennis team.

35. Marion Emery[10] (Wilfred Napoleon Emery[9], Jean (John) Baptist Emery Dit Coderre[8], Luc Emery Dit Coderre[7], Luc Emery Dit St. Luc[6], Joseph Emery Dit Coderre[5] Joseph Emery Dit Coderre[4], Antoine Emery Dit Coderre[3], Magny Aymeric Emery[2], Emery Dit Coderre[1]) was born on May 27, 1918[284] in Yorkville, New York and died on November 16, 1995 in Albany Medical Center, Albany, New York[285] . She married Armand Ramaccia on December 30, 1947 in St. Paul's Church, Whitesboro, New York, the son of Tarquinio "Frank" Ramaccia and Angronata "Carrie" Garafalo. He was born on October 02, 1919 in Sherburne, New York [286] and died on September 02, 2006 in Swanton, Vermont[287]. Marion was a graduate of Whitesboro High School. She was a member of St. Paul's Church, Whitesboro, where she had been active in the choir and other church activities. Armand lived in Sherburne, New York where his father worked in the knitting mills and died of tuberculosis in 1921 when Armand was two years old. At that point his mother moved the family to Norwich. He attended Norwich High School and participated in many activities and sports including basketball, golf, boxing and football. He was most proud of his football career at Norwich. He was a starter on the varsity team his junior and senior years. During his junior year Norwich football set an all time league record that still stands today: undefeated, untied, and unscored upon. After high school, he

attended Utica Aircraft School where he graduated as a certified aircraft mechanic in November 1941. One month before Pearl Harbor. He was immediately called upon and served the war years in Hawaii from 1942-1945. On his journey to Hawaii, his troop ship was stalked by Japanese submarines and had to take evasive maneuvers for three days. He had been employed by Chicago Pneumatic. He retired after almost 40 years as a skilled mechanical and electrical technician. Marion Emery and Armand Ramaccia had three children who may still be living.

Photo of Marion Emery from the collection of Richard Emery and used with permission.

---

[284] Obituary Utica Newspaper, November 17, 1995
[285] Obituary Utica Newspaper, November 17, 1995
[286] Obituary Utica Newspaper, September 3, 2006
[287] Obituary Utica Newspaper, September 3, 2006

36. Charles Henry Emery[10] (Wilfred Napoleon Emery[9], Jean (John) Baptist Emery Dit Coderre[8], Luc Emery Dit Coderre[7], Luc Emery Dit St. Luc[6], Joseph Emery Dit Coderre[5] Joseph Emery Dit Coderre[4], Antoine Emery Dit Coderre[3], Magny Aymeric Emery[2], Emery Dit Coderre[1]) was born on December 14, 1919 in Yorkville, New York[288] and died on October 23, 2001 in Waterville, New York[289]. He married Lucille Patricia LaShombe on January 17, 1942 in St. John's Church, Utica, New York, the daughter of Fred LaShombe and Charlotte Santimow. She was born on March 17, 1921 in Utica, New York[290] and died on May 23, 2007 in St. Elizabeth Medical Center, Utica, New York[291]. Charles was a graduate of Whitesboro High School. As a member of the 31st Engineers Battalion of the U.S. Army, he served in Europe, Africa and the Middle East during World War II and received an honorable discharge in 1945. He and his wife moved to Waterville in 1945. Charles was a superintendent at International Heater, a supervisor at Chicago Pneumatic, a foreman for the Town of Augusta and retired as plant operator from the Oneida County Department of Public Works in 1984. Lucille was a graduate of Whitesboro High School. She attended St. Bernard's Church, Waterville, New York. Charles Henry Emery and Lucille Patricia LaShombe had six children who may still be living.

37. Wilfred L. Emery[10] (Wilfred Napoleon Emery[9], Jean (John) Baptist Emery Dit Coderre[8], Luc Emery Dit Coderre[7], Luc Emery Dit St. Luc[6], Joseph Emery Dit Coderre[5] Joseph Emery Dit Coderre[4], Antoine Emery Dit Coderre[3], Magny Aymeric Emery[2], Emery Dit Coderre[1]) was born on October 21, 1923 in New York Mills, New York and died on December 03, 2005 in Milwaukee, Wisconsin[292]. He was married on November 27, 1942 in Chippawa Falls, Wisconsin. At the time of his death, "Wiff" had nine grandchildren, six great grandchildren, and two step grandchildren and one step great granddaughter. His last residence was Monomonee Falls, Waukesha County, Wisconsin. Wilfred L. Emery and his wife had four children who may still be living.

---

[288] Obituary Utica Newspaper, October 24, 2001
[289] Obituary Utica Newspaper, October 24, 2001
[290] Obituary Utica Newspaper, May 24, 2007
[291] Obituary Utica Newspaper, May 24, 2007
[292] Obituary Menomonee Falls, Wisconsin

38. Raymond George Zimmer[10] (Laura L. Emery[9], (Jean (John) Baptist Emery Dit Coderre[8], Luc Emery Dit Coderre[7], Luc Emery Dit St. Luc[6], Joseph Emery Dit Coderre[5] Joseph Emery Dit Coderre[4], Antoine Emery Dit Coderre[3], Magny Aymeric Emery[2], Emery Dit Coderre[1]) was born on February 29, 1924 in Utica, New York[293] and died May 21, 2009 in Syracuse, New York[294]. He was married May 24, 1947 in St. Paul's Church, Whitesboro, New York. Raymond graduated from Whitesboro High School and Colorado State Teachers College. He served in the U.S. Army Air Corps during World War II and was responsible for repairing damaged sheet metal on the planes. For many years, he was employed as a purchasing agent and inside sales manager with Alling & Cory Printing and Industrial Paper Supply Company in Utica. He retired in 179. He was a parishioner of Our Lady of Lourdes Church in Syracuse and a former member o Sacred Heart Church in Utica and St. Patrick's Church in Boonville, New York. He was also a member of the American Legion Post 1113 in Whitesboro. He was an avid fisherman and bowler and served as secretary of his bowling league. Raymond George Zimmer and his wife have five children who may still be living.

Photo of Raymond Zimmer from the collection of Richard Emery and used with permission.

39. Doris Josephine Emery[10] (Alfred P Emery[9], (Jean (John) Baptist Emery Dit Coderre[8], Luc Emery Dit Coderre[7], Luc Emery Dit St. Luc[6], Joseph Emery Dit Coderre[5] Joseph Emery Dit Coderre[4], Antoine Emery Dit Coderre[3], Magny Aymeric Emery[2], Emery Dit Coderre[1]) was born on September 20, 1916 in Utica, New York [295] and died on September 08, 2006 in the Folts Home, Herkimer, New York[296]. She married John Ladd on June 18, 1939 in Sacred Heart Church, Utica, New York[297]. He was born on October 19, 1910[298] and died on October 03, 1997[299]. Doris graduated from Whitesboro High School. She had been employed by Berger's Department Store and for Service Systems at the former UNIVAC. She was a member of St. John's Church in Newport, New York and after moving to Frankfort, had attended Sts. Peter and Paul Church. She was a former

[293] Obituary Utica Newspaper, May 22, 2007
[294] Obituary Utica Newspaper, May 22, 2007
[295] Obituary Utica Newspaper, September 9, 2006
[296] Obituary Utica Newspaper, September 9, 2006
[297] Wedding Announcement, Utica Newspaper
[298] Social Security Death Index at Ancestry.com
[299] Obituary of wife, Utica Newspaper, September 9, 2006

member of the Catholic Daughters of the Americas and Schuyler Senior Citizens. After her marriage, she and her husband resided in Utica, Schuyler and Newport prior to moving to Streamside Manor in Frankfort.   Doris Josephine Emery and John Ladd had two children who may still be living.

40. Winifred M. Emery[10] (Alfred P Emery[9], (Jean (John) Baptist Emery Dit Coderre[8], Luc Emery Dit Coderre[7], Luc Emery Dit St. Luc[6], Joseph Emery Dit Coderre[5] Joseph Emery Dit Coderre[4], Antoine Emery Dit Coderre[3], Magny Aymeric Emery[2], Emery Dit Coderre[1]) was born on December 21, 1919 in Utica, New York and died on February 10, 2002 in St. Luke's Memorial Hospital, New Hartford, New York[300]. She married Earl Woodward before 1940. He died in 1970. She married George A. Pflanz on November 08, 1969 in Schuyler, New York, the son of George Pflanz and Harriett Stuber. He was born on August 30, 1920 in Utica, New York[301] and died on October 22, 1996 in St. Luke's Memorial Hospital, New Hartford, New York[302]. Winifred was educated in the Whitesboro Central Schools. She had been employed by Hemstrought Bakery for over 40 years. She was a Catholic and a member of the American Legion Post #229 Auxiliary. George was a member of the Moravian Church of the Good Shepherd and before his retirement, was an attendant at the Utica Psychiatric Center. He served with the U.S. Army during WW II in Italy, France, and Germany and fought in the Battle of the Bulge. Winifred M. Emery and Earl Woodward had four children who may still be living.

41. John "Jack" D. Emery[10] (Alfred P Emery[9], (Jean (John) Baptist Emery Dit Coderre[8], Luc Emery Dit Coderre[7], Luc Emery Dit St. Luc[6], Joseph Emery Dit Coderre[5] Joseph Emery Dit Coderre[4], Antoine Emery Dit Coderre[3], Magny Aymeric Emery[2], Emery Dit Coderre[1]) was born on January 27, 1923 in Utica, New York[303] and died on July 20, 2003 in New York Mills, New York[304]. He was married on April 10, 1948. John had honorably served in the US Navy during WWII. He had been employed with Bockardt Heating in Utica and later with the Whitesboro School System. He was a life-long communicant of St. Thomas Church, New Hartford, New York. He had 11 grandchildren and 2 great grandchildren at the time of his death.   John "Jack" D. Emery and his wife had five children who may still be living.

[300] Social Security Death Index at Ancestry.com
[301] Obituary Utica Newspaper, October 23, 1996
[302] Obituary Utica Newspaper, October 23, 1996
[303] Obituary Utica Newspaper, July 21, 2003
[304] Obituary Utica Newspaper, July 21, 2003

42. Walter Sylvester Emery[10] (Otis A. Emery[9], (Jean (John) Baptist Emery Dit Coderre[8], Luc Emery Dit Coderre[7], Luc Emery Dit St. Luc[6], Joseph Emery Dit Coderre[5] Joseph Emery Dit Coderre[4], Antoine Emery Dit Coderre[3], Magny Aymeric Emery[2], Emery Dit Coderre[1]) was born on April 24, 1912 in Whitesboro, New York[305] and died on March 07, 1984 in St. Elizabeth's Hospital in Utica, New York[306]. He married Emma Marie Burrows after 1938. She was born in 1908 in New Fane, New York[307] and died on December 12, 1968 at 1136 Miller Street, Utica, New York. After the death of Emma, he married again on August 23, 1969 in Utica, New York. Walter was the twin to Genevieve. He received his education in Whitesboro Schools. He was employed at the Bendix Corp. and Genuine Auto Parts. He was of the Catholic faith.

Emma came to Utica in 1933 and was a member of St. Francis deSales Church, Utica, New York.

Walter Sylvester Emery and Emma Marie Burrows had the following children:
      i.   John F. Emery was born July 22, 1941 in Utica, New York[308] and died September 18, 1941 in Utica, New York[309].
      ii.   Living Emery
Walter Sylvester Emery and his second wife had one child who may still be living.

43. Genevieve Emery[10] (Otis A. Emery[9], (Jean (John) Baptist Emery Dit Coderre[8], Luc Emery Dit Coderre[7], Luc Emery Dit St. Luc[6], Joseph Emery Dit Coderre[5] Joseph Emery Dit Coderre[4], Antoine Emery Dit Coderre[3], Magny Aymeric Emery[2], Emery Dit Coderre[1]) was born on April 24, 1912 in Whitesboro, New York and died March 3, 2003 in Orleans, Barnstable, Massachusetts. She married George A. Schoen on August 16, 1934 in St Paul's Catholic Church, Whitesboro, New York[310], the son of Albert Schoen. He was born on January 15, 1914[311] and died on June 27, 1981 in Cape Cod Hospital, Hyannis, Massachusetts.[312]   Genevieve was a twin to Walter.

---

[305] Obituary Utica Newspaper, March 8, 1984
[306] Obituary Utica Newspaper, March 8, 1984
[307] Obituary Utica Newspaper, December 13, 1968
[308] Obituary Utica Newspaper, September 19, 1941
[309] Obituary Utica Newspaper, September 19, 1941
[310] Wedding Announcement, Utica Newspaper
[311] Family information from Dick Emery
[312] Family information from Dick Emery

Genevieve Emery and George A Schoen had the following child:

i.   Jacqueline Ann Schoen was born September 2, 1939 and died January 21, 2008 in Orleans, Barnstable, Massachusetts.[313]   Jacquelyn graduated from West Covina High School in West Covina, California in the class of 1957.   She was married twice.

Photo of Genevieve Emery, her husband, George A. Schoen and daughter, Jacqueline Ann Schoen from the collection of Richard Emery and used with permission.

44. Thomas Joseph Emery[10] (Otis A. Emery[9], (Jean (John) Baptist Emery Dit Coderre[8], Luc Emery Dit Coderre[7], Luc Emery Dit St. Luc[6], Joseph Emery Dit Coderre[5] Joseph Emery Dit Coderre[4], Antoine Emery Dit Coderre[3], Magny Aymeric Emery[2], Emery Dit Coderre[1]) was born on June 24, 1913 in Whitesboro, New York[314] and died on October 31, 1958 in St Luke's Hospital, Utica, New York[315]. He married Nellie Lillian Elmer on June 11, 1938 in St Paul's Catholic Church, Whitesboro, New York[316], the daughter of Jesse and Margaret Elmer. She was born on September 30, 1913 in Utica, New York[317] and died on July 31, 2002 in Utica, New York[318]. Thomas graduated from Whitesboro High School. He was a Veteran of World War II in the U.S. Coast Guard and participated in the D-Day Normandy invasion, carpenters mate. He had been employed by the Bendix Corporation as a foreman in the spare parts department. Nellie was named after her aunt Nellie (White) Davis. She enjoyed dancing and was active in square and round dancing for 25 years. She was also a member and past president of Chapter 15 of the Auxiliary to the Sons of the Union Veterans of the Civil War. Thomas Joseph Emery and Nellie Lillian Elmer had one child who is still living.

45. Irene Veronica Emery[10] (Otis A. Emery[9], (Jean (John) Baptist Emery Dit Coderre[8], Luc Emery Dit Coderre[7], Luc Emery Dit St. Luc[6], Joseph Emery Dit Coderre[5] Joseph Emery Dit Coderre[4], Antoine Emery Dit Coderre[3], Magny Aymeric Emery[2], Emery Dit Coderre[1]) was born on August 22, 1915 in Whitesboro, New York and died on December

[313] Family information from Dick Emery
[314] Obituary Utica Newspaper, November 1, 1958
[315] Obituary Utica Newspaper, November 1, 1958
[316] Wedding Announcement, Utica Newspaper
[317] Obituary Utica Newspaper, August 1, 2002
[318] Obituary Utica Newspaper, August 1, 2002

03, 1989 in Los Angeles, California[319]. She married Paul Lewis Ensworth on June 12, 1937 in St. Paul's Catholic Church Rectory, Whitesboro, New York[320]. He was born on September 27, 1913[321] and died on June 16, 1990 in San Diego, California[322]. Irene Veronica Emery and Paul Lewis Ensworth had one child who is still living.

46. Lorraine Emery[10] (Leo Anthony Emery[9], (Jean (John) Baptist Emery Dit Coderre[8], Luc Emery Dit Coderre[7], Luc Emery Dit St. Luc[6], Joseph Emery Dit Coderre[5] Joseph Emery Dit Coderre[4]**,** Antoine Emery Dit Coderre[3], Magny Aymeric Emery[2], Emery Dit Coderre[1]) was born on August 25, 1919 in Michigan[323] and died on June 29, 2002 in Mesa, Arizona[324]. She married George T. Benedict in 1938. He was born on April 22, 1916 in Ohio[325] and died on February 13, 1990 in Dexter, Michigan[326]. Lorraine Emery and George T. Benedict had three children who may still be living.

---

[319] California Death Index at Ancestry.com
[320] Wedding Announcement, Utica Newspaper
[321] Social Security Death Index at Ancestry.com
[322] Social Security Death Index at Ancestry.com
[323] Social Security Death Index at Ancestry.com
[324] Social Security Death Index at Ancestry.com
[325] Social Security Death Index at Ancestry.com
[326] Social Security Death Index at Ancestry.com

Chapter Two

Descendants of John Foote

Loyalty And Truth

Foote

In the old days Coats of Arms were often ordered struck and given to individuals by their king for acts of fortitude and fidelity. It was for such an act that James Foote was given the above "Arms."[1]

---

[1] Foote Family Association of America web page

Generation One

1. John Foote[1] was born in 1496 in Royston, Hertfordshire, England[2] and died on July 18, 1558 in Royston, Hertfordshire, England[3]. He married Helen Warren. She was born in 1500 in Bessingborn, Cambridgeshire, England[4] and died on July 18, 1558 in St Leonard, London, Middlesex, England[5].

John Foote and Helen Warren had the following child:
2.　　i.　　**Robert (John) Foote** was born in 1523 in Of, Royston, Hertfordshire, England[6] and died July 18, 1558 in Bessingborn, Cambridgeshire, England.

Generation Two

2. Robert (John) Foote of Royston[2] (John Foote[1]) was born in 1523 in Of, Royston, Hertfordshire, England[7] and died on July 18, 1558 in Bessingborn, Cambridgeshire, England[8]. He married Helen (Ellen) Waler (Warren) about 1548 in Of, Royston, Hertfordshire, England, the daughter of Richard Warren (Waller) and Alice Jenaway. She was born in 1527 in Of, Bessingborn, Cambridgeshire, England[9] and died in July 1559 in St. Leonard Chapel, London, Middlesex, England[10]. Robert Foote Royston was one of our oldest confirmed ancestors. He owned a small manor house along with some land in the Town of Royston.

Robert (John) Foote of Royston and Helen (Ellen) Waler (Warren) had the following children:
　　　i.　　Alice or Aves Foote was born about 1549 in Royston, Hertfordshire, England[11] and died in Royston, Hertford, England[12]. She married Mr. Sawle, about 1570.

---

[2] Ancestry.com, Public Member Trees for John Foote
[3] Ancestry.com, Public Member Trees for John Foote
[4] Ancestry.com, Public Member Trees for John Foote
[5] Ancestry.com, Public Member Trees for John Foote
[6] Family Search.org
[7] Family Search.org
[8] Family information from Wilma Fleming Haynes
[9] Family Search.org
[10] Family Search.org
[11] Family Search.org
[12] Family Search.org

ii.   Nathaniel Foote was born about 1551 in Of, Bessingborn, Cambridgeshire, England[13].

iii.   Elizabeth Foote was born about 1551 in Royston, Hertfordshire, England[14] and died after 1616 in Of, Royston, Hertfordshire, England[15]. She married Mr. Smith in1572 in Royston, Hertfordshire, England.

3.   iv.   Sir Robert Foote of Shalford was born in 1553 in Shalford, Colchester, Essex, England and died January 27, 1608 in Shalford, Essex, England[16].

v.   Thomas Foote was born in 1557 in Of, London, England[17].

vi.   John Foote was born in 1558 in Shalford, Essex, England[18] and died November 17, 1616 in Royston, Hertford, England[19]. He married Margaret Brooke in 1581 in Colchester, Essex, England, the daughter of John Brooke of London. She died in 1634[20]. John was a citizen and grocer of London. John Foote and Margaret Brooke had six children.

Generation Three

3. Sir Robert Foote of Shalford[3] (Robert (John) Foote[2], John Foote[1]) was born in 1553 in Shalford, Colchester, Essex, England[21] and died on January 27, 1608 in Shalford, Essex, England[22]. He married Joane Brooke on June 18, 1576 in St. Leonard Eastcheap, London, Middlesex, England, the daughter of John Brooke of London and Elizabeth Whetman (Waterman). She was born on June 18, 1555 in Of, London, Middlesex, England[23] and died on October 10, 1634 in St. Leonard, London, Middlesex, England[24].

Robert Foote of Shalford, a Yoeman in Old England was a Freeholder, next under the rank of Gentlemen, and in the early times one who owned a small landed estate. He owned property in Shalford and Royston.

---

[13] Family Search.org
[14] Family Search.org
[15] Family Search.org
[16] Family Search.org
[17] Family Search.org
[18] Family Search.org
[19] Family Search.org
[20] Foote Family Association of America Web Page
[21] Family Search.org
[22] Family Search.org
[23] Family Search.org
[24] Family Search.org

Last Will and Testament of Sir Robert Foote of Shalford:

Robert Foote, of Shalford, Essex, yeoman, 27 Jan., 1608, proved 15 Feb., 1608. To the poor in the parish twenty shillings. To the poor in Wethersfield twenty shillings. To my well beloved wife Joane, during her natural life, all such yearly rent as to me is reserved out of my lease of certain tenements which I hold for divers years yet enduring by the grant of Sir Robert Chester, knight, and lying and being in the town of Royston, the yearly rent whereof to me reserved is at this present eight pounds. I give her also one annuity of four pounds to be paid during her natural life to my son Robert. To my son James fifty pounds. To son Daniel forty pounds at four and twenty. The same each to sons Nathaniel, Francis, and Joshua at like ages. To daughter Elizabeth Foote forty pounds at day of marriage or at age of thirty. To son Joseph my lease and term of years in a certain hopground called Plomley which I hold by lease from Mr. Josyas Clarke and his wife. Other gists to him. Certain household stuff to wife. Elizabeth Ormes my maidservant. Tibbet, the wife of William Tibbet, five shillings in recompence of her pains she hath taken with me. To Mr. Richard Rogers preacher of God his Word twenty shillings. The wife of George Elsing. Thomas Cott. To my son Robert my free tenement or mansion house wherein I now inhabit, with the land, etc. and the stock of hop poles upon the ground, he to pay the legacies, etc. The residue of my goods etc. to all my children. If it happen my daughter Mary Hewes to be departed then her part to be paid to her children. For the execution of this will I do ordain, nominate and appoint my well beloved son Robert Foote to be my sole executor and I do desire my well beloved brother John Foote of London grocer and my son in law John Hewes of Royston to be supervisors and assistants to my executors. Dorset, 21.

Sir Robert Foote of Shalford and Joane Brooke had the following children:

    i.   Robert Foote was born in 1578 in Of, Shalford, Essex, England[25] and died September 04, 1646 in Cholchester, England[26]. He married Elizabeth Childe, the daughter of Wolstone Childe and Ellyne Empson. She was born about 1586 and was christened November 25, 1599 at St. Helen-Bishopsgate, London, England[27]. Robert was a grocer in London. Robert Foote and Elizabeth had three children.

    ii.   Mary Foote was born in 1584 in Shalford, Essex, England[28] and died February 14, 1602 in Shalford, Essex, England[29]. She married John Hewes of Royston on February 14, 1602[30]. He was born in 1583 and died in 1621[31]. Mary Foote and John Hewes of Royston had nine children.

[25] Family Search.org
[26] Family Search.org
[27] Foote Family History and Genealogy, Volume Two by Abram W. Foote
[28] Family Search.org
[29] Family Search.org
[30] Foote Family History and Genealogy, Volume Two by Abram W. Foote
[31] Foote Family Association of America Web Page

iii.   James Foote was born in 1587 in Shalford, Essex, England[32] and died in 1649 Colchester, Essex, England[33].   James Foote was an Iron Monger in London.

iv.   Elizabeth Foote was born in 1587 in Shalford, Essex, England[34] and died in 1651 in St. Leonards, Eastcheap, London, England[35].

v.   Daniel Foote was born in 1590 in St. Leonard's, Eastcheap, London, England[36] and died in 1641 in Colchester, Essex, England[37].   Daniel had no children.

vi.   Joseph Foote was born in 1590 in Shalford, Essex, England[38] and died in September 1639 in Colchester, Essex, England. He married a lady by the name of Anne. Joseph Foote and Anne had eight children.

4.   vii.   Nathaniel Foote, The Settler, was born September 21, 1592 in Shalford, Colchester, Essex, England[39],[40] and died November 20, 1644 in Wethersfield, Hartford, Connecticut[41].

vii.   Francis Daniel Foote was born in 1595 in Of, Colchester, Essex, England[42] and died December 15, 1624 in Colchester, Essex, England[43]. Francis lived in London and had no children.

ix.   Joshua Foote was born in 1600 in St. Leonard's Eastcheap, London, England[44] and died October 31, 1655 in Providence, Rhode Island[45]. Joshua Foote was an Iron Monger who lived in London, England until he moved to Roxbury, Massachusetts in the year 1650. He and his wife had four children who all lived in London and did not come to America.

---

[32] Family Search.org
[33] Family Search.org
[34] Family Search.org
[35] Family Search.org
[36] Family Search.org
[37] Family Search.org
[38] Family Search.org
[39] Family Search.org
[40] Foote Family Association of America Web Page
[41] Family Search.org
[42] Family Search.org
[43] Family Search.org
[44] Family Search.org
[45] Family Search.org

Generation Four

4. Nathaniel Foote, The Settler[4] (Sir Robert of Shalford Foote[3], Robert (John) Foote[2], John Foote[1]) was born on September 21, 1592 in Shalford, Colchester, Essex, England[46],[47] and died on November 20, 1644 in Wethersfield, Hartford, Connecticut[48]. He married Elizabeth Deming in January 1615 in Colchester, Essex, England, daughter of Johnathan Deming and Elizabeth Gilbert. She was born between 1595 and 1600 in Colchester, England[49] and died on July 28, 1683 in Wethersfield, Hartford, Connecticut[50].

The following was taken from the Foote Family Association Web Page:[51]

The story of Nathaniel Foote, the Settler

Nathaniel was born in St. Botolph's, Billingsgate, London, England. Accepted data from the period indicates that only a few colonists arrived in New England in the years immediately following the arrival of the Mayflower. It is known that in the spring of 1630, about 1500 people crossed the Atlantic in one expedition organized and led by John Winthrop, first Governor of Massachusetts Bay Colony. Soon after Governor Winthrop's 1630 expedition, Nathanial Foote, his family and his brothers, Pasco and John (or Caleb) decided to seek their fortunes in the New World. According to tradition, they left their homes in Colchester and sailed to Plymouth, Massachusetts, on the brig "Fortune".

Some sources say Nathaniel, his wife Elizabeth, and their six children settled in Watertown, Massachusetts. Pasco settled in Salem, Massachusetts, and it is not known where John (or Caleb) lived. As far as we know, John had no children. Nathaniel Foote, the first of this family in America, is of record in the Colony of Massachusetts Bay as early as 1633, in which year he took oath as a freeman. He was first of Watertown, and was among the first settlers of Wethersfield, Connecticut, receiving a distribution of land in the latter town in 1640. In 1644 he was deputy to the General Court. He was an intelligent, pious and industrious man. He was married in England in 1615, to Elizabeth

---

[46] Family Search.org
[47] Foote Family Association of America Web Page
[48] Family Search.org
[49] Family Search.org
[50] Family Search.org
[51] Foote Family Association of America Web Page

Deming, and died in Wethersfield in 1644. His widow married Thomas Welles, later governor of the Colony; she died July 28, 1683.

Nathaniel's Apprenticeship

Nathaniel Foote, The Settler resided in Shalford Parish, county Essex and St. Mary Bothaw Parish, London. At the age of sixteen he was apprenticed on September 21, 1608 to Samuel Croyle of Colchester, a "Grocer" and "Free Burgess", for a period of 8 years or until his 24th birthday in the year 1616. He was a grocer himself as of October 18, 1619, when he brought a message from Beatrice Barker, Esq., located on East Street, St. James Parish, Colchester. A short time after he finished his apprenticeship training, he was married to Elizabeth Deming (In January of the year 1616) in Colchester, Essex, England. She was the sister of John Deming, who was one of the first settlers of Wethersfield, Connecticut in the year of 1615. John Deming was for many years one of the magistrates of the "Colony of the Connecticut" and one of the Patentees named in its charter.

The Movement to America

Sometime before the year 1633 the family moved from London, England to Boston, Massachusetts and then Watertown, Massachusetts. About 1634 the General Court decided that they would allow people of Watertown to move to any place of their choice, provided they continue still under this Government. Consequently several adventurers including Nathaniel, his wife Elizabeth, and their six children ranging in age from sixteen year old Elizabeth to baby Sarah, and others decided to leave the Watertown Bay colony. They felt conditions around the Boston area had become too crowded. The group of adventurers, led by John Oldham, started a new settlement in the Connecticut wilderness. The new settlement was first called Pyquag. Later the name was changed to Wethersfield. He was also one of the first settlers of Wethersfield, Connecticut around the year 1635. According to the records of "The Original Distribution of Lands Around Wethersfield" recorded in 1640, a short time after arriving in Wethersfield in 1635, Nathaniel received a ten acre house lot on the east side of Broad Street. This land was near the south end of the street. Additionally, he became the owner of several other tracts laying in part in the great meadow east of his house and containing close to 400 acres of land. Note: Part of his land is now a public park at the foot of Broad Street.

Photo of the" Old Burial Ground" taken by the author in 2008 in Wethersfield, Connecticut.

Nathaniel's Profession

Even though Nathaniel's main profession in England was that of a crochet, he became a farmer. He was also active in the public trusts of the town. He was appointed as a delegate to the "General Court" in the year 1644. It is thought that Nathaniel may have taken part in the first public election held by American people held in Wethersfield on April 11, 1640. Remember the general court had stated they must "continue still under this Government." For the adventurers to hold public elections was a direct defiance of the Royal Courts of the Crown. This election took place 135 years before the Declaration of Independence in Philadelphia, Pennsylvania. Nathaniel Foote was the first cousin of Sir Thomas Foote, Sheriff of London in 1649 and Lord Mayo of London in 1650. Sir Thomas Foote was the son of Robert Foote of Royston and the brother of Robert Foote of Shalford, who was Nathaniel's Father. Records show that Nathaniel Foote died in Wethersfield, Connecticut in November 1644 at the age of 51. He was buried in the burying ground in the rear of the town meeting house, where nine generations are buried. Nathaniel was survived by his wife, two sons, and five daughters.

The Elizabeth Deming Story

Elizabeth Deming was born in England in the last part of the 16th Century. About 1615 she married Nathaniel Foote who had a grocery business in Cholchester, England. After the birth of their six children, Nathaniel decided to sell his grocery business and immigrate to the New World. By some he is considered to be the first settler of Wethersfield. Whether this is true or not, we do not know. We do know he was one of the

first ten men who settled along the bank of the Connecticut River and eventually named their settlement Wethersfield. They are now known as the Ten Adventurers. Nathaniel Foote was one of those names in the charger of patentees of Wethersfield. Between 1641 and 1644, he served as a Deputy to the General Assembly, as well as a member of the colony Grand Jury. The Foote family became one of the leading families of the little Connecticut Colony. He became a magistrate, a leading land owner, eventually owning more than 500 acres of land in Wethersfield, some of the great meadow, and his home on the south end of the green, next to the present Broad Street.

Photo of the Nathaniel Foote, the Settler Monument, and the author, at the end of Broad Street in Wethersfield Connecticut taken in 2008.

The family was saddened by Nathaniel's death at age 51. Elizabeth was so respected that she was allowed to be executor of his estate. Elizabeth was left a wealthy widow, but did not remain in that status for long. In 1646 she married Thomas Welles who was a widower with several children from his first marriage. Thomas Welles served as Governor of Connecticut Colony for two terms, 1655 - 1658. When he was not serving as governor, he was a Deputy Governor. He died during his last years of being Deputy Governor, January 14, 1659/1660. Elizabeth was again a widow, having two families instead of one. She was in control of a large estate from both husbands.

Elizabeth Welles was a tenacious and feisty old woman. She had not only survived a perilous voyage from England, but while tending to six exuberant children and a husband, she made a new life for herself and her family in a world they knew nothing about. This world was inhabited by Indians who were not always friendly with those pale face people. The rigors of life and managing a household did not daunt her. Things went quite well through the intervening years since arriving on shores of the newly discovered continent, until she reached old age. In 1676 as she approached the age of 80 years, she ran into trouble with one of her step-grandchildren. This was Robert Welles, a favorite of grandfather, Governor Thomas Welles, when the Governor was alive. Robert had arrived at the Governor's home, there to be taken care of and educated. But now his grandfather was dead and Robert and his step-grandmother disagreed. Maybe she did not think him old enough to be married at age 24. Never the less, it was 1676 when Elizabeth brought Robert Welles to court, because he ".hath dammyfield her barn by parting with the other part of the barn that did adjoin to it." Exactly what he did to her barn is not clear. The court's decision was clear. He was ordered to repair the barn and also to pay his step-grandmother rent for it. Elizabeth made sure the barn incident was not her last word. Two years later, in 1678, she made sure all the Welles' were taken care of when she made her will. She left them nothing. She stated someone outside the family would be executor of her will. Everything she had she left to her own family. That is the family she and Nathaniel had raised and nurtured. The Welles family got nothing. Elizabeth died in 1683, at the age of 88. The estate was divided among the Footes. One of the documents in the Probates Court was that of the final disposition, that during that same year Robert Welles won a lawsuit against his step-grandmother's will, that he would have to be paid by those who had been name in the will. John Deming, the brother of Elizabeth, was also one of the first settlers in Wethersfield, Connecticut. He was one of the patentees in its charter and for many years was one of the magistrates of the Colony of Connecticut.[52]

Nathaniel Foote and Elizabeth Deming had the following children:

      i.   Elizabeth Foote was born September 08, 1616 in Of Colchester, Essex, England[53] and died September 08, 1700 in Wethersfield, Hartford, Connecticut[54]. Elizabeth was baptized January 14, 1617 at St. James Parish Church, Colchester, England[55]. She married Josiah Churchill of Wethersfield Connecticut in 1638 in Wethersfield, Hartford, Connecticut. He died about January 1, 1686[56]. Elizabeth Foote and Josiah Churchill had seven children[57].

---

[52] "Foote Prints" Spring 1999 Issue from the Foote Family Association of America
[53] Foote Family History and Genealogy, Volume One by Abram W. Foote, page 23
[54] Foote Family History and Genealogy, Volume One by Abram W. Foote, page 23
[55] Foote Family History and Genealogy, Volume One by Abram W. Foote, page 23
[56] Foote Family History and Genealogy, Volume One by Abram W. Foote, page 23
[57] Foote Family History and Genealogy, Volume One by Abram W. Foote, page 23

5.   ii.   Nathaniel Foote Jr. was born in 1619 in Cholchester, Essex, England[58] and died June 1655 in Wethersfield, Hartford, Connecticut[59]. He was baptized March 5, 1619 at St. James Parish Church, Colchester, England[60].

   iii.   Mary Foote was born in 1623 in Of Shalford, Essex, England[61] and died in December 1684 in Wethersfield, Hartford, Connecticut[62]. She married John Stoddard in 1642 in Wethersfield, Hartford, Connecticut[63]. He died in December 1664[64]. In 1674 Mary married John Goodrich of Wethersfield, Connecticut[65]. He died in April 1680[66]. After the death of John Goodrich, she married Lieutenant Thomas Tracy of Norwich, Connecticut[67]. He died November 7, 1685[68]. Mary Foote and John Stoddard had eight children.

6.   **iv.**   **Robert Foote** was born December 08, 1627 in Wethersfield, Hartford, Connecticut[69] and died in 1681 in Branford, New Haven, Connecticut.[70]

   v.   Frances Foote was born in 1629 in East Bergholst, Suffolk, England[71] and died February 03, 1678 in Hatfield, Massachusetts[72]. She married John Dickinson in 1648[73]. He died in 1676. She then married Francis Barnard of Hartford, Connecticut and Hadley, Massachusetts in 1677[74]. He died February 3, 1689 at the age of 81[75]. Francis Foote and John Dickinson had ten children[76].

   vi.   Sarah Foote was born in 1632 in England[77] and died in1673[78]. She married Jeremiah Judson of Stratford in 1652, Connecticut, the son of William and Grace Judson[79]. Sarah Foote and Jeremiah Judson had six children.

---

[58] Foote Family History and Genealogy, Volume One by Abram W. Foote, page 23
[59] Family Search.org
[60] Foote Family History and Genealogy, Volume Two by Abram W. Foote
[61] Family Search.org
[62] Family Search.org
[63] Foote Family History and Genealogy, Volume One by Abram W. Foote, page 23
[64] Foote Family History and Genealogy, Volume One by Abram W. Foote, page 23
[65] Foote Family History and Genealogy, Volume One by Abram W. Foote, page 23
[66] Foote Family History and Genealogy, Volume One by Abram W. Foote, page 23
[67] Foote Family History and Genealogy, Volume One by Abram W. Foote, page 23
[68] Foote Family History and Genealogy, Volume One by Abram W. Foote, page 23
[69] Family Search.org
[70] US and International Marriage Records , 1560 to 1900 at Ancestry.com
[71] Family Search.org
[72] Family Search.org
[73] Foote Family History and Genealogy, Volume One by Abram W. Foote, page 23
[74] Foote Family History and Genealogy, Volume One by Abram W. Foote, page 23
[75] Foote Family History and Genealogy, Volume One by Abram W. Foote, page 23
[76] Foote Family History and Genealogy, Volume One by Abram W. Foote, page 25
[77] Family information from Wilma Fleming Haynes
[78] Foote Family History and Genealogy, Volume One by Abram W. Foote, page 25
[79] Foote Family History and Genealogy, Volume One by Abram W. Foote, page 25

vii.   Rebecca Foote was born in 1634 in Wethersfield, Hartford, Connecticut[80] and died April 06, 1701 in Hadley, Hampshire, Massachusetts[81]. She married Lieutenant Phillip Smith in 1657 in Hadley, Hampshire, Massachusetts, the son of Samuel Smith[82]. He died January 10, 1685 and legend has it that he was "murdered with a hideous witchcraft." On October 2, 1688, Rebecca married Major Aaron Cook of Windsor, Connecticut and Northamton, Massachusetts. He was born about 1610 and died September 5, 1690[83]. Rebecca Foote and Phillip Smith had eight children.

Generation Five

5. Nathaniel Foote Jr.[5] (Nathaniel Foote[4], Sir Robert of Shalford Foote[3], Robert (John) Foote[2], John Foote[1]) was born in 1620 in Colchester, Essex, England[84] and died in June 1655 in Wethersfield, Hartford, Connecticut[85]. He married Elizabeth Smith in 1646 in Wethersfield, Hartford, Connecticut, the daughter of Lieutenant Samuel Smith of Wethersfield, Connecticut and Hadley Massachusetts[86]. She was born on January 28, 1627 in Hadleigh, Suffolk, England[87] and died on December 16, 1668 in Hadley, Hampshire, Massachusetts [88].

Nathaniel Foote Jr and Elizabeth Smith had the following children:

7. i.   Nathaniel Foote (quartermaster) was born January 10, 1647 in Wethersfield, Hartford, Connecticut[89] and died January 12, 1703 in Wethersfield, Hartford, Connecticut[90]

ii.   Samuel Foote was born May 1, 1649[91] in Wethersfield, Hartford, Connecticut and died September 07, 1689 in Wethersfield, Hartford, Connecticut. He married Mary Merrick[92].

[80] Family Search.org
[81] Family Search.org
[82] Foote Family History and Genealogy, Volume One by Abram W. Foote, page 25
[83] Foote Family History and Genealogy, Volume One by Abram W. Foote, page 25
[84] Yates Publishing, U.S. and International Marriage Records, 1560-190 at Ancestry.com
[85] Foote Family History and Genealogy, Volume One by Abram W. Foote, page 27
[86] Foote Family History and Genealogy, Volume One by Abram W. Foote, page 27
[87] Family Search.org
[88] Family Search.org
[89] Wethersfield Vital Record Barbour Collection Book 1634 to 1868
[90] Family Search.org
[91] Foote Family History and Genealogy, Volume One by Abram W. Foote, page 28
[92] Foote Family History and Genealogy, Volume One by Abram W. Foote, page 28

iii.   Daniel Foote was born 1652[93] in Westfield, Massachusetts and died March 26, 1704 in Stratford, Connecticut.   He married a girl by the name of Sarah and the second marriage was to a girl by the name of Mary[94].

v.   Elizabeth Foote was born May 20, 1654 in Westfield, Massachusetts and died September 16, 1696 in Deerfield, Massachusetts. She married Daniel Belden on November 10, 1670, the son of William Belden of Wethersfield, Connecticut. Elizabeth Foote and Daniel Belden had fourteen children, all of whom were killed by Indians on September 16, 1696.

6. Robert Foote[5] (Nathaniel Foote[4], Sir Robert of Shalford Foote[3], Robert (John) Foote[2], John Foote[1]) was born on December 08, 1627 in Wethersfield, Hartford, Connecticut[95] and died in 1681 in Branford, New Haven, Connecticut.[96] He married Sarah Potter on August 06, 1659 in Of Stonington, New London, Connecticut, the daughter of William and Frances Potter. She was born on August 22, 1641 in Of, Wallingford, New Haven, Connecticut[97] and died on August 23, 1706 in Branford, New Haven, Connecticut.[98]

Robert Foote, son of Nathaniel Foote, The Settler, was of Wethersfield and later of what is now Wallingford, Connecticut, and in 1668 and thereafter until his death in 1681, of Branford, Connecticut. In 1686 his widow, Sarah, married Aaron Blachley, of Branford, and subsequently of Guilford, Connecticut. He is referred to as 1st Lieut. Robert Foote.

Robert Foote and Sarah Potter had the following children:

i.   Nathaniel Foote was born April 13, 1660 in New Haven, Connecticut[99] and died in 1714 in Branford, Connecticut.[100] He married Tabitha Bishop in 1688[101] in Connecticut. She was born in Connecticut in 1657[102] and died in 1715[103].

ii.   Sarah Foote was born February 12, 1662 in Of, Watertown, Litchfield, Connecticut[104]. She married Isaac Curtis in August 13, 1682[105,106] the son of Richard

---

[93] Foote Family History and Genealogy, Volume One by Abram W. Foote, page 28
[94] Foote Family History and Genealogy, Volume One by Abram W. Foote, page 28
[95] US and International Marriage Records , 1560 to 1900 at Ancestry.com
[96] US and International Marriage Records , 1560 to 1900 at Ancestry.com
[97] US and International Marriage Records , 1560 to 1900 at Ancestry.com
[98] Family Search.org
[99] Family Search.org
[100] US and International Marriage Records , 1560 to 1900 at Ancestry.com
[101] US and International Marriage Records , 1560 to 1900 at Ancestry.com
[102] US and International Marriage Records , 1560 to 1900 at Ancestry.com
[103] Foote Family History and Genealogy, Volume One by Abram W. Foote, page 28
[104] US and International Marriage Records , 1560 to 1900 at Ancestry.com
[105] Foote Family History and Genealogy, Volume One by Abram W. Foote, page 28
[106] US and International Marriage Records , 1560 to 1900 at Ancestry.com

Curtis of Wallingford, Connecticut. He was born in Massachusetts in 1658[107]. She later married Nathaniel How of Wallingford, Connecticut on August 6, 1714[108]. He was born in 1662[109] and died July 15, 1712[110]. He died February 12, 1723[111]. Sarah Foote and Isaac Curtis had nine children.

      iii.   Elizabeth Foote was born March 18, 1666 in New Haven, Connecticut[112] and died May 14, 1730 in Guilford, New Haven, Connecticut[113]. She married John Graves in January 12, 1684[114], the son of John Graves and Elizabeth Stillwell of East Guilford, Connecticut. John was born in 1658 in Connecticut[115] and died December 1, 1726[116]. Elizabeth Foote and John Graves had ten children.

      iv.   Joseph Foote was born March 06, 1664[117] in New Haven, Connecticut and died March 06, 1751 in Branford, New Haven, Connecticut[118]. He married Abigail Johnson in 1690[119], the daughter of John Johnson. She was born on April 09, 1670 in Connecticut[120]. He later married Sarah Rose of Bramford, Connecticut in 1710, the daughter of Deacon John Rose. She died on June 03, 1741. He then married Susannah Frisbie on September 08, 1741. She died on May 17, 1767. Joseph Foote and Abigail Johnson had seven children.

      v.   Samuel Foote was born May 14, 1668 in New Haven, Connecticut[121] and died in 1696 in Branford, New Haven, Connecticut[122]. He married Abigail Barker in 1694[123]. She was born in 1668[124].

8.   **vi.**   **John Foote** was born July 24, 1670 in Branford, New Haven, Connecticut[125] and died 1713 in Branford, New Haven, Connecticut[126]. He married a girl by the name of Mary.

---

[107] US and International Marriage Records , 1560 to 1900 at Ancestry.com
[108] US and International Marriage Records , 1560 to 1900 at Ancestry.com
[109] US and International Marriage Records , 1560 to 1900 at Ancestry.com
[110] Foote Family History and Genealogy, Volume One by Abram W. Foote, page 28
[111] Foote Family History and Genealogy, Volume One by Abram W. Foote, page 28
[112] Foote Family History and Genealogy, Volume One by Abram W. Foote, page 29
[113] Foote Family History and Genealogy, Volume One by Abram W. Foote, page 29
[114] US and International Marriage Records , 1560 to 1900 at Ancestry.com
[115] US and International Marriage Records , 1560 to 1900 at Ancestry.com
[116] Foote Family History and Genealogy, Volume One by Abram W. Foote, page 29
[117] Foote Family History and Genealogy, Volume One by Abram W. Foote, page 29
[118] Family Search.org
[119] US and International Marriage Records , 1560 to 1900 at Ancestry.com
[120] US and International Marriage Records , 1560 to 1900 at Ancestry.com
[121] US and International Marriage Records , 1560 to 1900 at Ancestry.com
[122] Family Search.org
[123] US and International Marriage Records , 1560 to 1900 at Ancestry.com
[124] US and International Marriage Records , 1560 to 1900 at Ancestry.com
[125] Family Search.org
[126] Family Search.org

vii.   Stephen Foote was born December 14, 1672 in Branford, New Haven, Connecticut[127] and died October 23, 1762 in Branford, New Haven, Connecticut[128,129]. Stephen was a twin to Isaac. He married Elizabeth Nash in 1702[130]. She was born in 1672[131]. He later married a Hannah Howd in 1739[132]. She was born in 1674.

viii.   Isaac Foote was born December 14, 1672 in Branford, New Haven, Connecticut[133] and died February 11, 1758. Isaac was a twin to Stephen. Isaac married Rebecca Dickerman who was born in 1672[134].

Generation Six

7. Nathaniel Foote (quartermaster)[6] (Nathaniel Foote Jr[5], Nathaniel Foote[4] Sir Robert of Shalford Foote[3], Robert (John) Foote[2], John Foote[1]) was born on January 10, 1647[135]in Wethersfield, Hartford, Connecticut[136] and died on January 12, 1703 in Wethersfield, Hartford, Connecticut[137]. He married Margaret Bliss on May 02, 1672 in Springfield, Massachusetts[138], the daughter of Nathaniel Bliss of Springfield, Massachusetts. She was born on November 12, 1649 in Springfield, Massachusetts[139] and died on April 03, 1745 in Colchester, Connecticut[140].

After his marriage, Nathaniel lived in Hatfield for two years and then moved to Springfield. Nathaniel was called into the service of his country against the Indians and was actively engaged in the bloody and successful attack on their encampment at the falls in Connecticut River, a few miles above Deerfield, since called Turner's Falls in commemoration of the brave Captain Turner, who commanded the expedition. From Springfield, Nathaniel removed to Stratford, where his house on one acre was located on Main Street directly east of the old burial ground near the Congregational Church. This

[127] Family Search.org
[128] US and International Marriage Records , 1560 to 1900 at Ancestry.com
[129] US and International Marriage Records , 1560 to 1900 at Ancestry.com
[130] US and International Marriage Records , 1560 to 1900 at Ancestry.com
[131] US and International Marriage Records , 1560 to 1900 at Ancestry.com
[132] US and International Marriage Records , 1560 to 1900 at Ancestry.com
[133] Connecticut Town Birth Records, pre 1870 (Barbour Collection) at Ancestry.com
[134] US and International Marriage Records , 1560 to 1900 at Ancestry.com
[135] Foote Family History and Genealogy, Volume One by Abram W. Foote, page 29
[136] Wethersfield Vital Record Barbour Collection Book 1634 to 1868
[137] The History of Ancient Wethersfield Connecticut, Volume II Genealogies and Biographies, page 328
[138] US and International Marriage Records , 1560 to 1900 at Ancestry.com
[139] US and International Marriage Records , 1560 to 1900 at Ancestry.com
[140] Family Search.org

lot he conveyed in March 1680 to Benjamin Lewis, having decided to move with his family to Branford, where in February 1679 he was admitted "a planter" of the town and a "home lot" was granted to him on condition that it should have a tenantable house built upon it within two years, and that he come to settle amongst us or else the lot would return to the town again. In pursuing his "manifest destiny" to migrate, Nathaniel conveyed his lot, with sundry other lots of which he had possessed, to Jonathan Pitman of Stratford, and moved to Wethersfield where he continued to reside until his death. Although previous to that event, he planned another removal to a new settlement begun under his enterprise at "Jeremy's Farm," since and now called Colchester on the road from Hartford to New London.

Nathaniel Foote purchased Colchester prior to 1699, at which time the town was incorporated, named, and its boundaries defined. Prior to this date, this territory of Colchester was merely the hunting grounds of the Mohegan Indians, and there is no evidence of any Indian villages in this section. It may be visualized as having been a vast, unbroken forest where the red man roamed in quest of game. The story goes that Nathaniel Foote, of Wethersfield, acting as an agent for a company of planters, paid a visit to Owaneco, who was then Sachem of the Mohegan's, with a view of purchasing the hunting grounds, and that, by hook or crook, procured a deed from the poor Indian for the equivalent of about a dollar and a half. Following the purchase, the town was incorporated and the settlement began. Foote started building a house on a choice bit of land reserved for him, but unfortunately died before the house was completed and before he had removed with his family to Colchester. This house has been miraculously preserved and is now the shrine of the local D.A.R. It is also interesting to note that the descendents of this same family are residing in Colchester today.

Nathaniel Foote House is the oldest standing house in Colchester. Nathaniel started building a new home for his wife and nine children in Colchester in 1699. Because of ill health he was not able to finish the house or move to the new settlement. His son, Nathaniel, completed it in 1702 shortly before his father died of "a lingering consumption (Sic)".

Photo of the house of Nathaniel Foote in Colchester, Connecticut taken by the author in 2008.

The senior Nathaniel's widow and four youngest children moved there later, where Margaret lived to be ninety five years old. The house is supposed to have stood near the First Church and burying grounds, a mile north of the present center. A century or so later it was moved to the Hartford Turnpike and used as a post office. In 1896 Mrs. Frederick G. Bock bought the property on Broadway where the little old building stood, neglected and fast going to decay. She had it repaired and placed on the end of it a bronze cast at the Brooklyn Navy Yard from metal salvaged from a man-of-war. It was oblong with thirteen white stars on a blue field and the figures "1702" in red. Mrs. Bock, who was a member of the Colonel Henry Champion Charter of the Daughters of the American Revolution, decided to present the old house to the D.A.R. In 1925 it was removed to its present location on Norwich Avenue next to the office of the Town Clerk. This site was given by Edward M. Dy, who also laid a cement foundation for the house, shingled, clap boarded and painted the house, put a beautiful fence around it, and planted shrubbery. With this start the members of the chapter were spurred on to restore the inside and to fill it with appropriate furniture and ornaments. This property is currently owned by the Bacon Academy Board of Trustees.

Nathaniel Foote (quartermaster) and Margaret Bliss had the following children:

     i.   Sarah Foote was born February 25, 1672 and died July 24, 1756[141]. She married Thomas Olcott in November 1691[142]. Sarah Foote and Thomas Olcott had ten children.

     ii.   Margaret Foote was born December 1, 1674[143].

---

[141] Foote Family History and Genealogy, Volume One by Abram W. Foote, page 30
[142] Foote Family History and Genealogy, Volume One by Abram W. Foote, page 30
[143] Foote Family History and Genealogy, Volume One by Abram W. Foote, page 30

iii.   Elizabeth Foote was born June 23, 1677[144]. She married Robert Turner in June 1701[145]. He died about 1745[146]. Elizabeth Foote and Robert Turner had eight children.

iv.   Mary Foote was born November 24, 1679 in Wethersfield, Hartford, Connecticut[147]. She married Daniel Rose Jr. on May 14, 1706, the son of Daniel Rose and Elizabeth Goodwin[148]. Daniel was born August 20, 1667[149]. Mary Foote and Daniel Rose had eight children.

v.   Nathaniel Foote was born September 09, 1682 in Wethersfield, Hartford, Connecticut[150]. He married Ann Clark and Hannah Coleman[151].

vi.   Ephraim Foote was born February 11, 1685 in Wethersfield, Hartford, Connecticut[152]. He married Sarah Chamberlain.

vii.   Josiah Foote was born September 27, 1688 in Wethersfield, Hartford, Connecticut[153] and died in December 1778[154]. Josiah married Sarah Wells in 1708 and she died August 3, 1766[155]. Josiah Foote and Sarah Wells had eleven children.

viii.   Joseph Foote was born December 28, 1690 in Wethersfield, Hartford, Connecticut[156]. He married Ann Clothier and Hannah Northam.

ix.   Eunice Foote was born May 10, 1694 in Wethersfield, Hartford, Connecticut[157]. On December 3, 1712 she married Michael Taintor Jr, the son of Michael and Mary Taintor[158]. He was born in September 1680 and died March 11, 1771[159]. Eunice Foote and Michael Taintor Jr. had eight children.

---

[144] Foote Family History and Genealogy, Volume One by Abram W. Foote, page 30
[145] Foote Family History and Genealogy, Volume One by Abram W. Foote, page 30
[146] Foote Family History and Genealogy, Volume One by Abram W. Foote, page 30
[147] Wethersfield Vital Record Barbour Collection Book 1634 to 1868
[148] Foote Family History and Genealogy, Volume One by Abram W. Foote, page 30
[149] Foote Family History and Genealogy, Volume One by Abram W. Foote, page 30
[150] Wethersfield Vital Record Barbour Collection Book 1634 to 1868
[151] Foote Family History and Genealogy, Volume One by Abram W. Foote, page 30
[152] Wethersfield Vital Record Barbour Collection Book 1634 to 1868
[153] Wethersfield Vital Record Barbour Collection Book 1634 to 1868
[154] Foote Family History and Genealogy, Volume One by Abram W. Foote, page 35
[155] Foote Family History and Genealogy, Volume One by Abram W. Foote, page 35
[156] Wethersfield Vital Record Barbour Collection Book 1634 to 1868
[157] Wethersfield Vital Record Barbour Collection Book 1634 to 1868
[158] Foote Family History and Genealogy, Volume One by Abram W. Foote, page 30
[159] Foote Family History and Genealogy, Volume One by Abram W. Foote, page 30

8. John Foote[6] (Robert Foote[5], Nathaniel Foote[4], Sir Robert of Shalford Foote[3], Robert (John) Foote[2], John Foote[1]) was born on July 24, 1670 in Branford, New Haven, Connecticut[160] and died in 1713 in Branford, New Haven, Connecticut[161]. He married Mary Palmer in 1696 in Branford, New Haven, Connecticut, the daughter of Micah Palmer and Elizabeth Bulkeley. She was born on May 25, 1673 in Branford, New Haven, Connecticut[162].

John Foote and Mary Palmer had the following children:

     i.   Samuel Foote was born in December 25, 1696 in Branford, New Haven, Connecticut.[163] He died young[164].

     ii.   Mary Foote was born in 1696 in Branford, New Haven, Connecticut and died May 07, 1758 in East Have, New Haven, Connecticut. [165] She married John Chedsey on February 8, 1715[166]. She later married Nathaniel Luddington[167]. Mary Foote and John Chedsey had three children.

     iii.   Elizabeth Foote was born in 1697 in Branford, New Haven, Connecticut[168] and died 1725 in Branford, New Haven, Connecticut[169]. In 1720 she married Caleb Parmele Jr. He died July 14, 1750[170]. Elizabeth Foote and Caleb Parmele Jr. had three children.

9.   **iv.**   **Dr. Thomas Foote** was born in 1699 in Branford, New Haven, Connecticut[171] and died December 19, 1776 in Waterbury, New Haven, Connecticut[172].

     v.   John Foote, Jr. was born in 1701 in Branford, New Haven, Connecticut and died January 26, 1777 in Wallingford, New Haven, Connecticut[173]. He married Elizabeth Frisbie and Abigale Frisbie[174].

     vi.   Samuel Foote was born in 1702 in Branford, New Haven, Connecticut[175]. Samuel died early in life[176].

---

[160] Foote Family History and Genealogy, Volume One by Abram W. Foote, page 32
[161] Foote Family History and Genealogy, Volume One by Abram W. Foote, page 32
[162] Family Search.org
[163] Connecticut Town Birth Records, pre 1870 (Barbour Collection) at Ancestry.com
[164] Foote Family History and Genealogy, Volume One by Abram W. Foote, page 32
[165] Family Search.org
[166] Foote Family History and Genealogy, Volume One by Abram W. Foote, page 32
[167] Foote Family History and Genealogy, Volume One by Abram W. Foote, page 32
[168] Family Search.org
[169] Foote Family History and Genealogy, Volume One by Abram W. Foote, page 32
[170] Foote Family History and Genealogy, Volume One by Abram W. Foote, page 32
[171] Connecticut Town Birth Records, pre 1870 (Barbour Collection) at Ancestry.com
[172] Connecticut Town Birth Records, pre 1870 (Barbour Collection) at Ancestry.com
[173] Family Search.org
[174] Foote Family History and Genealogy, Volume One by Abram W. Foote, page 32
[175] Family Search.org

vii.   Jonathan Foote was born in 1704 in Branford, New Haven, Connecticut[177] and died June 27, 1754 in Waterbury, New Haven, Connecticut[178]. He married Lydia Shutliff[179].

viii.   Patience Foote was born in 1706 in Branford, New Haven, Connecticut[180]. On January 13, 1726, she married Daniel Palmer, Jr.[181] Patience Foote and Daniel Palmer Jr. had two children.

Generation Seven

9. Dr. Thomas Foote[7] (John Foote[6], Robert Foote[5], Nathaniel Foote[4], Sir Robert of Shalford Foote[3], Robert (John) Foote[2], John Foote[1]) was born in 1699 in Branford, New Haven, Connecticut[182] and died on December 19, 1776 in Waterbury, New Haven, Connecticut[183]. He married Elizabeth Sutliff about 1722 in Watertown, Litchfield, Connecticut[184], the daughter of John Sutliff and Hannah Brocket. She was born in 1708 in Waterbury, New Haven, Connecticut[185] and died on November 16, 1789 in Watertown, Litchfield, Connecticut[186].

Dr. Thomas Foote and Elizabeth Sutliff had the following children:

i.   Samuel Foote was born in 1723 in Watertown, Litchfield, Connecticut[187] and died June 09, 1776[188]. He married Mary Lyon on June 05, 1750[189].

ii.   Jemima Foote was born in 1725 in Watertown, Litchfield, Connecticut[190] and died May 20, 1779 in Waterbury, New Haven, Connecticut[191]. She married Abraham

[176] Foote Family History and Genealogy, Volume One by Abram W. Foote, page 32
[177] Family Search.org
[178] Connecticut Town Death Records, pre 1870 (Barbour Collection) at Ancestry.com
[179] Foote Family History and Genealogy, Volume One by Abram W. Foote, page 32
[180] Family Search.org
[181] Foote Family History and Genealogy, Volume One by Abram W. Foote, page 32
[182] Foote Family History and Genealogy, Volume One by Abram W. Foote, page 41
[183] Foote Family History and Genealogy, Volume One by Abram W. Foote, page 41
[184] Family Search.org
[185] Foote Family History and Genealogy, Volume One by Abram W. Foote, page 41
[186] Foote Family History and Genealogy, Volume One by Abram W. Foote, page 41
[187] Family Search.org
[188] Family Search.org
[189] Foote Family History and Genealogy, Volume One by Abram W. Foote, page 41
[190] Family Search.org
[191] Family Search.org

Hickox of Waterbury, Connecticut on April 19, 1748 in Branford, New Haven, Connecticut[192]. Jemima Foote and Abraham Hickox had nine children.

iii.   Elizabeth Foote was born in 1728 in Watertown, Litchfield, Connecticut[193] and died February 16, 1807 in Waterbury, New Haven, Connecticut[194]. She married Noah Griggs of Waterbury, Connecticut on May 26, 1765 in Waterbury, New Haven, Connecticut[195]. He died December 12, 1812[196]. Elizabeth Foote and Noah Griggs had three children.

iv.   Ebenezer Foote was born in 1730 in Of, Cornwall, Addison, Vermont[197] and died December 23, 1763 in Waterbury, Connecticut[198]. He married Martha Moss on June 17, 1752 in Waterbury, New Haven, Connecticut.

v.   Timothy Foote was born in 1735 in Cornwall, Addison, Vermont[199] and died May 08, 1799[200]. He married Mary Garnsey on June 05, 1755. He later married Lucy Wheeler[201].

10.   vi.   Dr. Nathan Foote was born January 25, 1738 in Waterbury, New Haven, Connecticut[202] and died July 25, 1808 in Charlotte, Vermont[203].

vii.   Thomas Foote was born May 10, 1740 in Waterbury, New Haven, Connecticut[204] and died February 18, 1803[205]. He married Rebecca Dowd on May 17, 1762 in Waterbury, New Haven, Connecticut. He later married Ann Adams[206].

viii.   Captain John Foote was born August 24, 1742 in Waterbury, New Haven, Connecticut[207] and died July 05, 1809[208]. He married Esther Matton on July 26, 1764 in Waterbury, New Haven, Connecticut[209], the daughter of David Matton. She was born on November 20, 1742 in Wallingford, New Haven, Connecticut[210] and died on March 10, 1769. He then married Mary Peck on July 20, 1769 in Hartford, Southington,

---

[192] Foote Family History and Genealogy, Volume One by Abram W. Foote, page 41
[193] Foote Family History and Genealogy, Volume One by Abram W. Foote, page 41
[194] Foote Family History and Genealogy, Volume One by Abram W. Foote, page 41
[195] Foote Family History and Genealogy, Volume One by Abram W. Foote, page 41
[196] Foote Family History and Genealogy, Volume One by Abram W. Foote, page 41
[197] Family Search.org
[198] Connecticut Town Death Records, pre 1870 (Barbour Collection) at Ancestry.com
[199] Family Search.org
[200] Family Search.org
[201] Foote Family History and Genealogy, Volume One by Abram W. Foote, page 41
[202] Connecticut Town Birth Records, pre 1870 (Barbour Collection) at Ancestry.com
[203] Foote Family History and Genealogy, Volume One by Abram W. Foote
[204] Connecticut Town Birth Records, pre 1870 (Barbour Collection) at Ancestry.com
[205] Family Search.org
[206] Foote Family History and Genealogy, Volume One by Abram W. Foote, page 41
[207] Connecticut Town Birth Records, pre 1870 (Barbour Collection) at Ancestry.com
[208] Foote Family History and Genealogy, Volume One by Abram W. Foote
[209] Foote Family History and Genealogy, Volume One by Abram W. Foote, page 72
[210] Family Search.org

Connecticut[211], the daughter of Gideon Peck. She was born about 1745 in Waterbury, New Haven, Connecticut[212] and died on November 22, 1822 in Ogdensburg, New York[213]. John Foote was a Captain in the Revolutionary War. Captain John Foote and Esther Matton had eleven children.

Generation Eight

10. Dr. Nathan Foote[8] (Dr. Thomas Foote[7], John Foote[6], Robert Foote[5], Nathaniel Foote[4], Sir Robert of Shalford Foote[3], Robert (John) Foote[2], John Foote[1]) was born on January 25, 1738 in Waterbury, New Haven, Connecticut[214] and died on July 25, 1808 in Charlotte, Vermont[215,216]. He married Marvia (Mavina) Selkrigg on June 12, 1759, the daughter of William Selkrigg of Waterbury Connecticut[217]. She was born on January 08, 1739[218] in Of Waterbury, New Haven, Connecticut[219] and died on September 26, 1814 in Cornwall, Vermont[220]. Dr. Nathan Foote died in Vermont at the home of his son, Uri. Dr. Nathan Foote came from Waterbury, Connecticut in 1774 and was the first settler in the town of Cornwall, Vermont. He was driven back by the Indians and went to Watertown, Connecticut for five years returning with his family to Cornwall, Vermont after the war. Nathan was a surgeon and served in the War of the Rebellion.

Dr. Nathan Foote and Marvia (Mavina) Selkrigg had the following children:

     i.   Daniel Foote was born April 03, 1760 in Waterbury, New Haven, Connecticut[221] and died August 24, 1848 in Cornwall, Vermont[222]. He married Sarah Johnson on September 11, 1783 and later married Ellen Scott[223]. Daniel was in the War of the Revolution for five years and served his country faithfully and was in many actions, the taking of Burgoyne, etc.

---

[211] Foote Family History and Genealogy, Volume One by Abram W. Foote
[212] Family Search.org
[213] Foote Family History and Genealogy, Volume One by Abram W. Foote, page 72
[214] Family Search.org
[215] Foote Family History and Genealogy, Volume One by Abram W. Foote
[216] Historical Society, Madison County, New York
[217] Foote Family History and Genealogy, Volume One by Abram W. Foote, page 71
[218] Connecticut Town Birth Records, pre 1870 (Barbour Collection) at Ancestry.com
[219] DAR papers from Mary Gregg Sperry
[220] Historical Society, Madison County, New York
[221] Connecticut Town Birth Records, pre 1870 (Barbour Collection) at Ancestry.com
[222] Family Search.org
[223] Foote Family History and Genealogy, Volume One by Abram W. Foote, page 72

ii.   Nathan Foote Jr was born November 16, 1761 in Waterbury, New Haven, Connecticut[224] and died November 16, 1828 in Cornwall, Vermont[225]. He married Sarah Evarts Sutherland in 1790, the daughter of Sylvanus Evarts and Elishaba Chittenden. She was born in April 1, 1764 and died September 1, 1804 in Cornwall, Vermont[226]. He later married Hester Goodrich Hunt in 1805. She was born about 1765 in Georgia, Vermont[227]. Nathan Foote Jr. and Sarah Evarts had six children.

iii.   Millicent Foote was born November 06, 1763 in Cornwell, Addison, Vermont[228] and died August 15, 1802 in Lincoln, Addison, Vermont[229]. She married Jedediah Durfee of Cornwall, Vermont in1783[230]. Millicent and Jedediah Durfee had six children.

iv.   Abijah Foote was born March 23, 1766 in Waterbury, New Haven, Connecticut[231] and died September 22, 1795 in Cornwall, Addison, Vermont[232]. He married Polly Bronson in 1703. She was born in 1770 in Woodbury, Litchfield, Connecticut[233] and died in Cornwall, Addison, Vermont[234]. Abijah Foote and Polly Bronson had one child.

v.   Uri Foote was born July 12, 1768 in Waterbury, New Haven, Connecticut[235] and died April 30, 1841 in Cayuga County, New York[236]. [237].He married Rhoda Pierson in 1798[238]. She was born about 1772 in Sherburn, Chittenden, Vermont[239]. Uri Foote and Rhoda Pierson had three children.

vi.   Jesse Foote was born September 17, 1770 in Waterbury, New Haven, Connecticut[240] and died December 07, 1772 in Clarendon, Rutland, Vermont[241].

vii.   Marian Foote was born November 06, 1772 in Clarendon, Vermont[242] and died April 04, 1798[243]. She married Asher Omstead of Cornwall, Vermont in February 1795[244]. Marian Foote and Asher Omstead had one child.

---

[224] Connecticut Town Birth Records, pre 1870 (Barbour Collection) at Ancestry.com
[225] Family Search.org
[226] Family Search.org
[227] Family Search.org
[228] Foote Family History and Genealogy, Volume One by Abram W. Foote, page 72
[229] Foote Family History and Genealogy, Volume One by Abram W. Foote, page 72
[230] US and International Marriage Records , 1560 to 1900 at Ancestry.com
[231] Connecticut Town Birth Records, pre 1870 (Barbour Collection) at Ancestry.com
[232] Ancestry.com, Public Member Trees for Abijah Foote
[233] Ancestry.com, Public Member Trees for Abijah Foote
[234] Foote Family History and Genealogy, Volume One by Abram W. Foote, page 72
[235] Connecticut Town Birth Records, pre 1870 (Barbour Collection) at Ancestry.com
[236] Family Search.org
[237] Foote Family History and Genealogy, Volume One by Abram W. Foote, page 72
[238] Foote Family History and Genealogy, Volume One by Abram W. Foote, page 72
[239] Family Search.org
[240] Foote Family History and Genealogy, Volume One by Abram W. Foote, page 72
[241] Foote Family History and Genealogy, Volume One by Abram W. Foote, page 72

11.   viii.   Jesse Selkrigg Foote was born May 17, 1776 in Rutland, Cornwall, Vermont[245] and died May 21, 1848 in Chittenango, New York[246].

ix.   Thomas Foote was born July 09, 1778 in Rutland, Vermont[247], and died September 03, 1819. He was lost at sea.[248].

x.   William Foote was born September 05, 1780 in Waterbury, New Haven, Connecticut[249] and died January 26, 1815 in St. Albans, Franklin, Vermont[250]. He married Patty Janes in 1806. She was born about 1784 in St. Albans, Franklin, Vermont[251]. William Foote and Patty Janes had two children.

xi.   Parthenia M. Foote was born May 05, 1784 in Cornwall, Vermont[252]. She lived in Cayuga, New York in 1846.

Generation Nine

11. Jesse Selkrigg Foote[9] (Dr. Nathan Foote[8], Dr. Thomas Foote[7], John Foote[6], Robert Foote[5], Nathaniel Foote[4], Sir Robert of Shalford Foote[3], Robert (John) Foote[2], John Foote[1]) was born on May 17, 1776 in Rutland, Cornwall, Vermont[253] and died on May 21, 1848 in Chittenango, New York[254]. He married Abigail Hosley in October 11, 1803, Salisbury, Vermont[255]. She was born about May 1776 in Salisbury, Addison, Vermont[256] and died on November 03, 1818 in Smithfield, New York[257]. He later married Eliza Denis in 1821 in Chittenango, New York[258]. She was born about 1780 in Waterbury,

[242] Foote Family History and Genealogy, Volume One by Abram W. Foote, page 72
[243] Foote Family History and Genealogy, Volume One by Abram W. Foote, page 72
[244] Foote Family History and Genealogy, Volume One by Abram W. Foote, page 72
[245] Foote Family History and Genealogy, Volume One by Abram W. Foote, page 72
[246] "Pioneers of Madison County"
[247] Foote Family History and Genealogy, Volume One by Abram W. Foote, page 72
[248] Foote Family History and Genealogy, Volume One by Abram W. Foote, page 72
[249] Family Search.org
[250] Family Search.org
[251] Foote Family History and Genealogy, Volume One by Abram W. Foote, page 183
[252] Foote Family History and Genealogy, Volume One by Abram W. Foote, page 72
[253] Foote Family History and Genealogy, Volume One by Abram W. Foote, page 72
[254] "Pioneers of Madison County"
[255] Marriage record from Salisbury, Vermont
[256] Family Search.org
[257] Family Search.org
[258] Foote Family History and Genealogy, Volume One by Abram W. Foote, page 182

New Haven, Connecticut[259] and died on March 13, 1839 in New York State[260]. Jesse Foote was a farmer by occupation. He served in the U.S. Forces in the War of 1812.

Jesse Selkrigg Foote and Abigail Hosley had the following children:

i.   Alphanso Foote was born in 1803 in Eaton, Madison, New York[261]. He was married in 1828 in Eaton, Addison, Vermont.   He raised a family.

ii.   Nathan Foote was born about 1804 in Bridgeport, Madison, New York[262]. He raised a family.

12.   iii.   Denice (Dennis) Foote was born in 1805 in Bridgeport, New York[263] and died in 1886 in Steuben County, New York[264].

13.   iv.   Hiram Foote was born February 18, 1806 in Bridgeport, New York[265] and died in December 1840 in Greigsville, Livingston, New York[266].

14.   v.   Joseph Hosley Foote was born September 10, 1811 in Eaton, New York[267] and died May 20, 1895 in Vernon, New York[268].

vi.   William Foote was born in 1813 in Eaton, New York[269].

vii.   Harvey Foote was born in March 1814 in Eaton, New York[270] and died September 18, 1814[271].

15.   **viii.**   **George L. Foote Sr.** was born July 15, 1818 in Town of Eaton, Madison County, New York[272,273] and died March 03, 1911 in Madison, New York[274].

---

[259] Family Search.org
[260] Family Search.org
[261] Family Search.org
[262] Family Search.org
[263] 1855 Madison County Census, Town of Sullivan
[264] Foote Family History and Genealogy, Volume One by Abram W. Foote
[265] Family Search.org
[266] E-mail from great great granddaughter, Mary Ingram Hill 4/14/2010
[267] Foote Family History and Genealogy, Volume One by Abram W. Foote, page 315
[268] Foote Family History and Genealogy, Volume One by Abram W. Foote, page 315
[269] Family Search.org
[270] Davis Farm Cemetery Record, Madison County, New York
[271] Davis Farm Cemetery Record, Madison County, New York
[272] Foote Family History and Genealogy, Volume One by Abram W. Foote, page 183
[273] Civil Ward Pension Records on George L. Foote, Sr.
[274] Madison Center Cemetery Records, Madison, New York

Generation Ten

12. Denice (Dennis) Foote[10] (Jesse Selkrigg Foote[9], Dr. Nathan Foote[8], Dr. Thomas Foote[7], John Foote[6], Robert Foote[5], Nathaniel Foote[4], Sir Robert of Shalford Foote[3], Robert (John) Foote[2], John Foote[1]) was born in 1805 in Bridgeport, New York[275] and died in 1886 in Steuben County, New York[276]. He married Elizabeth (Betsy) Conrad (Conroyd) on February 22, 1832 in Madison County, New York[277]. She was born in 1806 in Canada[278] and died before 1886[279]. The 1850 Madison County Census listed Dennis as a carpenter. In 1860 he lived in Chittenango, New York.

Denice (Dennis) Foote and Elizabeth (Betsy) Conrad (Conroyd) had the following child:
16.   i.   William H. Foote was born in 1834 in Madison County, New York[280].

13. Hiram Foote[10] (Jesse Selkrigg Foote[9], Dr. Nathan Foote[8], Dr. Thomas Foote[7], John Foote[6], Robert Foote[5], Nathaniel Foote[4], Sir Robert of Shalford Foote[3], Robert (John) Foote[2], John Foote[1]) was born on February 18, 1806 in Bridgeport, New York[281]. He died in 1840 in Greigsville, Livingston, New York[282]. He married Belinda Riley on February 03, 1828 in Salina, Onondaga, New York. She was born on March 29, 1809 in Salina, New York[283] and died on January 18, 1861 in Syracuse, New York[284].

Madison Observer - September 10, 1823

Foot, Hiram age, abt. 17 yrs, bound as a shoemaker, ran away from Benjamin H. Wilber of Peterboro.

Hiram Foote and Belinda Riley had the following children:
        i.   Edgar Foote was born December 13, 1828 in Syracuse, New York[285] and died February 14, 1905[286].

---

[275] 1855 Madison County Census, Town of Sullivan
[276] Foote Family History and Genealogy, Volume One by Abram W. Foote, page 183
[277] Vital Statistics from Chittenango, NY Newspapers, 1831-1854, page 19
[278] 1855 Madison County Census, Town of Sullivan
[279] Foote Family History and Genealogy, Volume One by Abram W. Foote
[280] 1855 Madison County Census, Town of Sullivan
[281] Family Search.org
[282] Family Search.org
[283] Family Search.org
[284] Family Search.org
[285] Family Search.org

      ii.   Delia Foote was born July 09, 1830 in Syracuse, New York[287] and died January 06, 1897[288].

      iii.   George Foote was born November 01, 1833 in Greigsville, Livingston, New York[289].

      iv.   Hellen Foote was born March 13, 1836 in Greigsville, Livingston, New York[290].

17.   v.   Hiram Foote Jr. was born June 03, 1838 in Greigsville, Livingston, New York[291] and died October 06, 1917 in Syracuse, New York[292].

14. Joseph Hosley Foote[10] (Jesse Selkrigg Foote[9], Dr. Nathan Foote[8], Dr. Thomas Foote[7], John Foote[6], Robert Foote[5], Nathaniel Foote[4], Sir Robert of Shalford Foote[3], Robert (John) Foote[2], John Foote[1]) was born on September 10, 1811 in Eaton, Madison, New York[293] and died on May 20, 1895 in Vernon, New York[294]. He married Rhoda (Rody) Esther Mason on July 31, 1835, the daughter of Harry Mason of Pompey, New York. She was born on March 09, 1816 in Madison County, New York[295] and died on December 08, 1903 in Town of Eaton, Madison County, New York[296]. The 1855 Madison County, Town of Eaton, Census said Joseph was a farmer. The 1868-69 Town of Eaton Directory showed Joseph as a farmer in Morrisville, Town of Eaton. Rody was listed as a border in the 1900 Madison County census, Town of Stockbridge. Rebecca Moon was the head of the household.

Joseph Hosley Foote and Rhoda (Rody) Esther Mason had the following children:

18.   i.   Milton Mason Foote was born June 27, 1840 in New York State[297].

19.   ii.   Helen Viola Foote was born November 22, 1845 in Morrisville, Madison County, New York[298] and died January 24, 1926 in Munnsville, New York[299].

---

[286] Family Search.org
[287] Family Search.org
[288] Family Search.org
[289] Family Search.org
[290] Family Search.org
[291] Family Search.org
[292] E-mail from great great granddaughter, Mary Ingram Hill 4/14/2010
[293] Foote Family History and Genealogy, Volume One by Abram W. Foote, page 315
[294] Oneida Post, Oneida, New York Saturday, May 25, 1895
[295] DAR papers from Mary Gregg Sperry
[296] Foote Family History and Genealogy, Volume One by Abram W. Foote, page 315
[297] Foote Family History and Genealogy, Volume One by Abram W. Foote, page 315
[298] Obituary. Oneida Daily Dispatch, January 29, 1926
[299] Obituary. Oneida Daily Dispatch, January 29, 1926

15. George L. Foote Sr[10] (Jesse Selkrigg Foote[9], Dr. Nathan Foote[8], Dr. Thomas Foote[7], John Foote[6], Robert Foote[5], Nathaniel Foote[4], Sir Robert of Shalford Foote[3], Robert (John) Foote[2], John Foote[1]) was born on July 15, 1818 in Town of Eaton, Madison County, New York[300] and died on March 03, 1911 in Madison, New York[301]. George died at 4:10 PM of bronchial pneumonia. He married Abigail Ann Webb on January 21, 1841. She was born in 1820 in Delaware County, New York[302] and died on July 20, 1858 in Madison, New York[303]. He married Lydia M. Leigh on December 11, 1859 in Madison, New York, the daughter of William T. and Lydia M. Leigh. She was born on January 30, 1839 in Onondaga County, New York[304] and died on March 30, 1886 in Oriskany, New York[305]. He married Catherine Carey Price on October 29, 1882 in Ithaca, Michigan[306]. She was born in May 1844 in Ohio[307] and died on June 04, 1926 in New Berlin, New York.

The 1850 Census listed George as a butcher. He was 39 years old, Abigale was 24, William was 4, and Mary A. was 1 year old. The 1855 Madison, New York Census listed George as a butcher, and was married to Abigale and had children William, age 9, and Mary, age 5. The Census indicated they had lived in Madison for 5 years. The 1860 Census said he owned land and was a farmer. The Morrisville Observer indicated his hotel was going to be auctioned off to the highest bidder on January 25, 1873 for default on his mortgage. There was a notice in the December 29, 1875 issue of the Morrisville Observer that George had been fined $40 for selling liquor on Sunday, so perhaps he was able to pay his mortgage and keep the hotel. The 1880 Madison Census says George Foote was a hotel keeper and listed the following people living with George and Lydia: Jay D. Foot, Charles Foot, Earl Foot, Mary Hull, (age 57), Albert Fitch (age 46), Burton Gifford (age 23), William Darrow (age 28), and Nellie Bohan (age 22). This may have been when he was the proprietor of the Madison Hotel and the people listed, other than his children, were most likely employees or residents of the hotel.

---

[300] Civil Ward Pension Records on George L. Foote, Sr
[301] Civil Ward Pension Records on George L. Foote, Sr
[302] Madison Center Cemetery Records, Madison, New York
[303] Civil Ward Pension Records on George L. Foote, Sr
[304] Death Certificate
[305] Death Certificate
[306] Michigan Birth Records
[307] 1900 Michigan Census, Town of Lyons, County of Ionia, District 17

Map of Madison Village in 1874. The G. L. Foote Hotel is located in the center of town at the crossroad of Main Street and Hamilton Street.

The 1900 Census indicated George lived in Lyons, Ionia County, Michigan and in the 1910 Census; he lived on West Street in Madison, New York.

July 27, 1904 - Utica Paper

George L. Foote of Pompeii, Michigan arrived in Madison for a visit with his family. He stayed with his son, William. He had not been home in 18 years.

George apparently left his wife, Lydia, and his children, and moved to Michigan about 1881. They were all together in the 1880 census, but he married again in 1882 in Michigan. Lydia was alive in the 1880 Census but stated she was sick at that time with Rheumatism. Lydia moved to Whitestown in 1883 and sold the Oriskany Hotel. George had apparently left her in 1881 or 1882, as he married again in 1882 in Michigan. Lydia died of consumption and pneumonia in 1886. There were seven notices in the Rome Citizen newspaper looking for George, as three of his children were minors when their mother died.   The notices were dated: April 16, 1886, April 23, 1886, April 30, 1886, May 7, 1886, May 14, 1886, May 21, 1886 and May 28, 1886.

Born 1818
died 1911
9 3 yrs

Y. EVENING, JULY 27, 19

38 IN FAMILY REUNION.

Relatives Meet After Eighteen Years —Take Steamer Ride.

George L. Foote of Pompeii, Mich., arrived in Madison Friday for a visit of several months with his son, William Foote of that village. Mr. Foote was a resident of Madison village about thirty years ago. Twenty-two years ago he removed to Michigan and has since made that State his home. Yesterday there gathered at the old home his sons and daughter with their children and grandchildren. Among those present were Mrs. Mary A. Mather and Miss Gertie Mather of Whitesboro, Mr. and Mrs. Lynn Foote and daughters Agnes, Isabel and Edna of Utica; Mr. and Mrs. Charles L. Foote and son Stewart, Earl Foote and Miss Laura Rudd of Canastota; Miss Clara Foote of Buchanan, Mrs. Morris O'Connell and daughter Helen of Cortland; and Mr. and Mrs. William Foote of Madison. Mr. Foote had not seen his children in over eighteen years and the meeting was a most enjoyable one, especially as it was not expected that so many would be present. Only one son, Jay D. Foote of South Fallsburg, was absent. Several pictures were taken, one being of Mr. Foote, his son, William Foote, and daughter, Mrs. Mather; two granddaughters, Mrs. Morris O'Connell and Miss Gertie Mather, and two great-grandchildren, Miss Laura Rudd and Miss Helen O'Connell.

Mr. Foote is over 86 years old, and though very feeble, made the journey from Michigan to Madison alone. Thirty-eight relatives were present besides a number of other guests. Today the entire party is cruising on Madison Lake.

Notice in the Utica Newspaper of George Foote's return to Madison, New York for a visit.

Taken from Pioneers of Madison County

George L. Foote was born in Madison County in 1818, proprietor of Foot's Hotel at Eaton 1878. His wife, Abigail, died in 1857. George engaged in farming following the Civil War and later disposed of his farm and purchased the Madison Hotel, which he ran for number of years. After he sold the hotel, he moved to Michigan where he again took up farming. He lived in Madison, New York after his retirement.

THE SYRACUSE HERALD SUNDAY MORNING, JULY 26, 190?.

REMARKABLE DOUBLE FOUR GENER-
ATIONS OF THE FOOTE FAMILY

Photo found in the Syracuse Herald on July 26, 1908. This four generation picture was taken on George's 90th birthday. The people in the picture are: George is in the middle and to his right is his oldest daughter, Mary Abigale Mather, her daughter, Mrs. Annie Rudd and granddaughter, Iva. To his left is his oldest son, William H. Foote, and his daughter Mrs. Millie O'Conner and granddaughter, Helen.

Obituary - Waterville Times, March 10, 1911

The funeral of George Foote was held at his home Monday afternoon. He was 93 years of age and had been in poor health for some time. He was a member of the G.A.R. Post.

Obituary - Madison County Leader, Morrisville, NY March 9, 1911

George L. Foote of Madison died at his late home on Friday, aged 93 years. He was born in the town of Smithfield in the year 1818, where he lived until early manhood, when he took up his residence at Syracuse where he entered the canal boating traffic between Buffalo and New York over the Erie Canal. A few years later he moved to Madison and went into the butchering and meat business. He followed this vocation for a number of years and when the Civil War broke out he enlisted in the Union forces and served throughout the conflict, and was honorably discharged. He then returned to Madison and purchased a farm at Madison Center, which he conducted for several years, when he sold the property and purchased the Madison Hotel. A few years later he disposed of the hotel and moved to Michigan and again took up farming. After a number of years in Michigan he returned to Madison, some six or seven years since. He has since lived a retired life. He had been three times married, and is survived by his widow and one son William H.

GEORGE L. FOOTE.

Foote, of Madison, and a daughter Mrs. Mary A. Mather of Whitesboro; G.L. Foote of Utica, J.D. Foote of Cooks Falls, Charles Foote and Earl Foote of Canastota. The funeral services were held from his late home on Monday afternoon at 1 o'clock, burial being made in the village cemetery.

Photo of George L. Foote from his obituary.

In the 1860 Census, Lydia was 17 years old and had been married to George within the last year. The 1865 Census indicated Lydia was born in Onondaga County and an Ann Lee, age 14, born in Otsego County, was living with them. In the 1870 Census Lydia was married to George and with them lived John Lee, age 21 and Annie Lee, age 19. Lydia sold the Oriskany Hotel to Mr. Carr on May 5, 1884 and moved to Railroad Street in Oriskany, New York[308].

George L. Foote Sr and Abigail Ann Webb had the following children:

20.   i.   William H. Foote was born April 03, 1846 in Onondaga County, New York[309] and died March 21, 1938 in Cortland, New York[310].

---

[308] Utica, New York Observer, May 6, 1884
[309] Obituary Utica Newspaper, March 22, 1938
[310] Obituary Utica Newspaper, March 22, 1938

21.   ii.   Mary Abigale Foote was born June 26, 1849 in Onondaga County, New York[311] and died March 03, 1913 in Whitesboro, New York[312].

Photo of Mary Abigale Foote Mather from the collection of Kerry Cannon and used with permission.

George L. Foote Sr. and Lydia M. Leigh had the following children:

   i.   Agnes E. Foote was born November 24, 1861 and died January 20, 1862[313]

22.   **ii.**   **George L. Foote Jr.** was born January 15, 1863 in Madison, New York[314] and died June 14, 1945 in Utica, New York.[315]

   iii.   Jay Dean Foote was born January 07, 1870 in Madison, New York[316] and died August 21, 1923 in Cooks Falls, New York[317]. He married Lizzie Dolaway on January 15, 1903 in Jersey City, New Jersey. The Abram Foote Genealogy book indicates Jay was born January 7, 1874 and was a twin to Charles L. Foote. I found no other documentation to prove this.

Obituary - The Sullivan County Review, Thursday, August 30, 1923 J. D. Foote

On Tuesday evening, August 21st at 11:30, J.D. Foote of Cooks Falls passed away quietly at his home. People were shocked at this news, for, while it was known that Mr. Foote had been ailing for months, his death was unlooked for. Jay Dean Foote was born at Madison, NY January 7th, 1870, the second son of George Foote and Lydia Lee Foote. He is survived by three brothers, a half brother and a stepmother and by his widow Lizzie Dolaway Foote whose former home was South Fallsburgh, and to whom he was married in Jersey City on January 15th, 1903. He has been station agent at Cook's Falls for over sixteen years and was employed by the O. and W. Railroad for approximately

---

[311] Foote Family History and Genealogy, Volume One by Abram W. Foote, page 315
[312] Obituary Utica Newspaper, March 4, 1913
[313] Madison Cemetery List from DAR
[314] Obituary Utica Newspaper, June 15, 1945
[315] Obituary Utica Newspaper, June 15, 1945
[316] Obituary Sullivan County Review, August 30, 1923
[317] Obituary Sullivan County Review, August 30, 1923

twenty-five years. He was a member of the Brotherhood of O.R.T. and a man of sterling qualities who will be sadly missed by hosts of friends.

Jay lived in Cooks Falls, New York in 1908 and did not have any children.

23.   iv.   Charles Lewis Foote was born January 04, 1874 in Madison, New York[318] and died December 17, 1950 in Oneida City Hospital, Oneida, New York[319].

24.   v.   Earl James Foote was born March 12, 1878 in New York State[320] and died November 20, 1971 in Canastota, New York[321].

George L. Foote Sr. and Catherine Carey Price had the following child:

    i.   Glenn L. Foote was born on January 26, 1884 in Dallas, Clinton, Michigan[322]. Glen did not register in the World War I draft registration. He may have died young.

Civil War Journey

George L. Foote served in Company A, 176th Regiment New York State Volunteers in the Civil War.

Company A was recruited principally from Hamilton, Madison, Brookfield, and Canastota, New York to serve for nine months. On December 22, 1862, Colonel Hoyt's regiment received the designation 176th Infantry, and was mustered into the service of the United States at New York City.

The Civil War records on George L. Foote, age 44, enlisted November 5, 1862 at Madison to serve 9 months. He mustered in as a private in Co. A. November 26, 1862. George was captured in action June 23, 1863 at Brashear City, Louisiana and was held prisoner[323]. The following is a chart of the missing, wounded and killed in the 176th Regiment[324].

---

[318] World War I draft registration on Ancestry.com
[319] Obituary, Oneida Daily Dispatch, December 18, 1950
[320] World War I draft registration on Ancestry.com
[321] Obituary, Oneida Daily Dispatch
[322] Michigan Birth Records
[323] Civil War Pension papers of George L. Foote
[324] *New York in the War of the Rebellion*, 3rd ed. Frederick Phisterer

PLACE.	Date.	Killed.		Wounded.				Missing.		Aggregate.
				Died.		Recov'd.				
		Officers.	Enlisted men.	Officers.	Enlisted men.	Officers.	Enlisted men.	Officers.	Enlisted men.	
	1863.									
Pattersonville, La.	June 17-19	....	1	....	....	....	....	....	....	1
La Fourche Crossing, La.	19-21	....	2	....	2	....	11	....	1	16
Thibodeaux, La.	20	....	....	....	....	....	....	....	10	10
Fort Buchanan, La.	23	} 1	3	....	6	....	2	19	406	437
Bayou Boeuff, La.	23									
Brashear City, La.	23-24	....	....	....	....	....	....	....	....	....
	1864.									
Red River Campaign, La.	March 10- May 22									
Mansura	May 16	....	....	....	....	....	....	....	1	1
Simsport	19	....	1	....	....	....	....	....	....	1
Berryville, Va.	Sept. 8	....	....	....	....	1	....	....	....	1
Opequon, Va.	19	....	5	....	3	3	27	....	9	47
Fisher's Hill, Va.	22	....	1	....	....	....	1	....	....	2
Cedar Creek, Va.	Oct. 19	1	6	....	1	4	10	1	30	53
	1865.									
Campaign of the Carolinas	March- April 26	} ..	....	....	....	....	....	....	....	....
Bennett House, N.C.	April 26									
Total loss		2	19	....	12	7	52	20	457	569

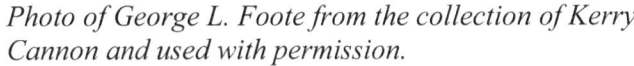

Muster role of 176th Volunteer Infantry

There was no parole date mentioned, but George mustered out with the company November 20, 1863 at New York City, 176th Volunteer Infantry. Following his discharge from the Civil War, he lived in Madison, New York for 18 years. In 1881 he moved to Michigan. He stayed in Michigan for 25 years. At the time of his marriage to Catherine Price, they lived in Maple Rapids, Michigan. He subsequently moved back to Madison, New York where he died.

Photo of George L. Foote from the collection of Kerry Cannon and used with permission.

Generation Eleven

16. William H. Foote[11](Denice (Dennis) Foote[10], Jesse Selkrigg Foote[9], Dr. Nathan Foote[8], Dr. Thomas Foote[7], John Foote[6], Robert Foote[5], Nathaniel Foote[4], Sir Robert of Shalford Foote[3], Robert (John) Foote[2], John Foote[1]) was born in 1834 in Madison County, New York[325]. He married a girl by the name of Julia. In the 1860 Chittenango, New York Census, William was listed with a wife and two children. His parents lived next door. William was found in the 1880 Addison, Steuben County, New York census living with his parents. A daughter, Effa M. Foote was living with them also.

William H. Foote and Julia had the following children:
  i.   Julia E. Foote was born in 1858 in New York State[326].
  ii.   Effa M. Foote was born in1860 in New York State[327].

17. Hiram Foote Jr[1] (Hiram Foote[10], Jesse Selkrigg Foote[9], Dr. Nathan Foote[8], Dr. Thomas Foote[7], John Foote[6], Robert Foote[5], Nathaniel Foote[4], Sir Robert of Shalford Foote[3], Robert (John) Foote[2], John Foote[1]) was born on June 03, 1838 in Greigsville, Livingston County, New York[328] and died on October 06, 1917 in Syracuse, New York[329].

Hiram enlisted as a Musician on May 13, 1861, at the age of 23, into Company C, 12th Infantry Regiment, New York. He enlisted as a Drummer in the Civil War and was promoted to Full Drum Major on September 1, 1861. He was discharged from Company C, 12th Infantry Regiment New York on 28 Oct 1862 at Antietam, Maryland[330]. He enlisted a second time into the 185th Regiment New York Infantry Volunteers on September 5, 1864 and was discharged May 30, 1865 at Washington, D.C. He was 5 feet 6 inches tall with blue eyes and light hair and complexion[331].

Photo of Hiram Foote Jr. when he was enlisted in the Army during the Civil War. From the collection of Mary Ingram Hill and used with permission.

---

[325] 1855 Madison County Census, Town of Sullivan
[326] 1860 Chittenango, New York Census
[327] 1880 Town of Addison, Steuben, New York Census
[328] Family Search.org
[329] Family Search.org
[330] American Civil War Soldiers at Ancestry.com
[331] Civil War papers on Hiram Foote

He married Mary Dorothea Balz in December 15, 1863 at J. O. Filmore Park Central Church, Syracuse, New York[332]. She was born in 1845 in Prussia, Germany[333] and died August 25, 1913 in Syracuse, New York[334]. Hiram was listed in the 1910 Syracuse Census, Ward 1, as retired. He was a well know baker in the Syracuse area.

Hiram Foote Jr. and Mary Dorothea Balz had the following children:

25.   i.   Charles Jacob Foote was born in September 19, 1864 in New York State[335] and died in August 30, 1904[336].

ii.   Hiram Foote III was born in September 9, 1864 in New York State[337]. The 1910 Syracuse Census, Ward 1, listed Hiram as single and working in a bake shop. The 1930 Census showed Hiram living in the Onondaga Home and Hospital in Syracuse, New York.

iii.   Julia Foote was born in August 5, 1868 in New York State[338]. The 1910 Syracuse Census, Ward 1, listed Julia as single and working in a dressmaker shop.

18. Milton Mason Foote[11] (Joseph Hosley Foote[10], Jesse Selkrigg Foote[9], Dr. Nathan Foote[8], Dr. Thomas Foote[7], John Foote[6], Robert Foote[5], Nathaniel Foote[4], Sir Robert of Shalford Foote[3], Robert (John) Foote[2], John Foote[1]) was born on June 27, 1840 in Morrisville, New York[339]. He married Louise C. Coman on December 12, 1866[340]. She was the daughter of Orvilliers Coman of Eaton, New York. She died March 17, 1869[341]. He later married Clara Elizabeth Reed March 21, 1870, the daughter of Josiah Reed of Deruyter, New York[342]. She was born in 1849 in New York State[343]. The 1860 and 1870 Madison County Census for the Town of Eaton indicated Milton was a printer. In 1880 Milton was found in the Watertown, New York Census. He lived in Syracuse in 1885.

---

[332] Civil War papers on Hiram Foote
[333] Family Search.org
[334] Civil War papers on Hiram Foote
[335] E-mail from great great granddaughter, Mary Ingram Hill 4/14/2010
[336] Death notice, Syracuse Telegram, August 31, 1904
[337] Civil War papers on Hiram Foote
[338] Civil War papers on Hiram Foote
[339] Foote Family History and Genealogy, Volume One by Abram W. Foote, page 446
[340] Foote Family History and Genealogy, Volume One by Abram W. Foote, page 446
[341] Foote Family History and Genealogy, Volume One by Abram W. Foote, page 446
[342] Foote Family History and Genealogy, Volume One by Abram W. Foote, page 446
[343] 1880 Watertown, New York Census

Milton Mason Foote and Clara Elizabeth Reed had the following children:

26.   i.   Coleman M. Foote was born in February 13, 1868 in New York State[344]. He married Etta M. Brown.

        ii.   Harry Foote was born March 12, 1874 in New York State[345]. He married Elma Hull[346].

        iii.   Alice Louise Foote was born in April 4, 1876 in Oswego, New York[347]. She married Frank C. Wiltsie of Marcellus, New York on December 8, 1897[348]. He was a farmer and poultry fancier. Alice Louise Foote and Frank C. Wiltsie had two children.

        iv.   Fred Foote was born in August 25, 1878 in Watertown, New York[349]. He married Cora E. Smith, the daughter of George H. Smith of Syracuse, New York on June 4, 1903[350]. His occupation was listed as a photographer artist in Syracuse, New York.

27.   v.   Elmer Mason Foote was born April 08, 1886 in Syracuse, New York[351] and died July 16, 1973 in Community Memorial Hospital, Hamilton, New York[352].

19. Helen Viola Foote[11] (Joseph Hosley Foote[10], Jesse Selkrigg Foote[9], Dr. Nathan Foote[8], Dr. Thomas Foote[7], John Foote[6], Robert Foote[5], Nathaniel Foote[4], Sir Robert of Shalford Foote[3], Robert (John) Foote[2], John Foote[1]) was born on November 22, 1845 in Munnsville, Madison County, New York[353] and died on January 24, 1926 in Munnsville, New York[354]. She married Edwin G. Sanford on February 01, 1865. He died on March 09, 1875[355]. She later married Nathaniel Milton Gregg on October 28, 1877. He was born on March 12, 1833 in New York State and died on February 17, 1912 in Munnsville, New York[356]. The 1910 Madison County, Town of Stockbridge, Census listed Helen as a school teacher. She lived with her daughter in the 1920 Census in Stockbridge Township, Madison, County, New York. Helen had been a school teacher in the town of Stockbridge for many years. Edwin Sanford was from Oneida Castle, New York.

---

[344] Foote Family History and Genealogy, Volume One by Abram W. Foote, page 446
[345] Foote Family History and Genealogy, Volume One by Abram W. Foote, page 446
[346] Foote Family History and Genealogy, Volume One by Abram W. Foote, page 446
[347] Foote Family History and Genealogy, Volume One by Abram W. Foote, page 446
[348] Foote Family History and Genealogy, Volume One by Abram W. Foote, page 446
[349] Foote Family History and Genealogy, Volume One by Abram W. Foote, page 446
[350] Foote Family History and Genealogy, Volume One by Abram W. Foote, page 446
[351] World War I draft registration on Ancestry.com
[352] Obituary Syracuse Newspaper, July 17, 1973
[353] Foote Family History and Genealogy, Volume One by Abram W. Foote, page 315
[354] Will of Helen Foote Gregg
[355] Foote Family History and Genealogy, Volume One by Abram W. Foote, page 315
[356] New York State Vital Records

Helen Viola Foote and Edwin G. Sanford had the following child:

　　　i.　　Louis E. Sanford was born January 13, 1868 in Oneida Castle, New York[357]. Louis was living with his mother and step father at the age of 39 in the 1910 census. No occupation was listed.

Helen Viola Foote and Nathaniel Milton Gregg had the following child:

　　　i.　　Mary Esther Gregg was born December 23, 1880 in Munnsville, New York[358] and died February 20, 1961 in Oneida City Hospital, Oneida, New York[359]. She married John Arthur Sperry, October 10, 1907[360]. Mary was noted in the Munnsville area as a leader in the Women's Club and a civic leader for many years. She was a member of St. John's Episcopal Church, Oneida, New York; Skenandoah Chapter, Daughters of the American Revolution, the Bethlehem White Shrine; past Matron of Achmetha Chapter 422, Order of Eastern Star; past Noble Grand of Nyanda Rebekah Lodge; and chairman of the Munnsville Chapter of the Red Cross for 30 years. She did not have children.

20. William H. Foote [11] (George L. Foote Sr[10], Jesse Selkrigg Foote[9], Dr. Nathan Foote[8], Dr. Thomas Foote[7], John Foote[6], Robert Foote[5], Nathaniel Foote[4], Sir Robert of Shalford Foote[3], Robert (John) Foote[2], John Foote[1]) was born on April 03, 1846 in Onondaga County, New York[361] and died on March 21, 1938 in Cortland, New York[362]. William served in the Civil War in Company I, 157th New York Cavalry. This unit fought in the Battle of Gettysburg July 1-3, 1863, with Major General George Gordon Meade commanding the troupes. He married Anna Mariah Weaver on February 25, 1875[363]. She was born in 1845 in Stockbridge, New York and died on December 26, 1905[364]. He later married Mabel Kenyon who died in 1923[365]. Lastly he married a lady by the name of Mary L. who died in December 5, 1924 in Madison, New York[366]. William was a carpenter and joiner by trade.

[357] Foote Family History and Genealogy, Volume One by Abram W. Foote, page 315
[358] Obituary, Oneida Daily Dispatch, October 11, 1907
[359] Obituary, Oneida Daily Dispatch, October 11, 1907
[360] Obituary, Oneida Daily Dispatch, October 11, 1907
[361] Obituary Utica Newspaper, March 22, 1938
[362] Madison Center Cemetery, Madison, New York
[363] Foote Family History and Genealogy, Volume One by Abram W. Foote, page 446
[364] Obituary, Oneida Daily Dispatch, February 26, 1875
[365] Obituary of husband, Utica Newspaper, March 22, 1938
[366] Death Announcement, Utica Newspaper December 10, 1924

Taken from Obituary of William H. Foote

William H. Foote, 93, former resident of Utica and Madison and veteran of 46 engagements in the Civil War, died Monday at his home in Cortland. He lived in Utica and Madison until about a year ago when he removed to Cortland. Foote was in many important battles and several horses were shot under him, yet he never was wounded. He was at the siege of Harper's Ferry, Antietem, Fredericksburg, Gettysburg and Brandy Station and participated in the review of the Grand Army in Washington in May 1865. He was honorably discharged June 27, 1865 at Alexandria, Virginia. He was born at a small settlement near Syracuse, the son of the late Mr. & Mrs. George Foote. He enlisted in Utica in December 1861 in Company I, 157th New York Cavalry.

William H. Foote and Anna Mariah Weaver had the following children:

    i.   Clarence Foote was born February 21, 1876[367] and March 04, 1880[368].

    ii.   Clara E. Foote was born October 29, 1878 in Michigan[369], and died October 23, 1930 in Cortland, New York[370]. An obituary for Clara was not found in the Cortland paper. However the death notice stated she was the daughter of William.

    iii.   George H. Foote was born January 17, 1881 in Madison, New York[371] and died March 23, 1923[372]. He married Alice Henry on September 16, 1903[373]. George was found in the 1910 Census living at 154 Carroll Street, Binghamton, New York. He was listed as a mail carrier and had been married for six years and had no children at that time. He was still living in Binghamton in 1920 and had no children listed.

28.   iv.   Mildred (Nellie) E. Foote was born June 10, 1884[374] and died in 1964.

William H. Foote and Mary L. had the following children:

    i.   Katherine M. Foote married a man by the name of Kumming.

    ii.   Mrs. Charles Culver.

---

[367] Foote Family History and Genealogy, Volume One by Abram W. Foote
[368] Madison Center Cemetery Records, Madison, New York
[369] Madison Center Cemetery Records, Madison, New York
[370] New York State Vital Records
[371] Foote Family History and Genealogy, Volume One by Abram W. Foote
[372] Family Search.org
[373] Family Search.org
[374] Foote Family History and Genealogy, Volume One by Abram W. Foote

21. Mary Abigale Foote [11] (George L. Foote Sr[10], Jesse Selkrigg Foote[9], Dr. Nathan Foote[8], Dr. Thomas Foote[7], JohnFoote[6], Robert Foote[5], Nathaniel Foote[4] Sir Robert of Shalford Foote[3], Robert (John) Foote[2], John Foote[1]) was born on June 26, 1849 in Onondaga County, New York[375] and died on March 03, 1913 in Whitesboro, New York[376]. She married Herman D. Mather on June 12, 1873 in Utica, New York. He was born in 1845[377] and died on April 11, 1926 in G.A.R. Home, St. Johnsville, New York[378]. Abby Foote worked as a servant for the Julius Tucker family in 1865 in Madison, New York. She was a servant for Edwin R. Barker in Madison County Town of Eaton in 1870. Mary and Herman D. lived in Utica in 1880. Mary lived on Powell Road in Whitesboro in the 1910 Whitestown Census. That census indicated she had three children, two of which were living. Her obituary said she had two children and two grandchildren. In the 1900 Census, she lived with her daughter Anna in Lenox, Madison County, New York.

Photo of Mary Abigale Foote from the collection of Susan Whitman and used with permission.

Herman fought in the Civil War, Company E., 16th Regiment U.S. Infantry. The Canastota Directory for 1887 and 1888 indicated Herman was a night policeman and lived at Stocking Lane in Canastota.

Mary Abigale Foote and Herman D. Mather had the following children:

29.   i.   Anna Lydia Mather was born April 26, 1875 in Madison, New York[379] and died March 15, 1969 at 9 West Street, Whitesboro, New York[380].

30.   ii.   Gertrude M. Mather was born April 09, 1876 in Silome, New York and died May 06, 1963 in St. Luke's Memorial Hospital, New Hartford, New York[381].

iii.   George F. Mather was born April 09, 1879 in New York State[382] and died July 13, 1888[383]. "Georgie" is all that is on his tombstone.

---

[375] Foote Family History and Genealogy, Volume One by Abram W. Foote
[376] Obituary Utica Newspaper, March 4, 1913
[377] Mt. Pleasant Cemetery, Canastota, New York
[378] Death Announcement Utica Newspaper April 16, 1926
[379] Obituary Utica Newspaper, March 16, 1969
[380] Obituary Utica Newspaper, March 16, 1969
[381] Obituary Utica Newspaper, May 7, 1963
[382] Foote Family History and Genealogy, Volume One by Abram W. Foote
[383] Mt. Pleasant Cemetery, Canastota, New York

22. George L. Foote Jr.[11] (George L. Foote Sr.[10], Jesse Selkrigg Foote[9], Dr. Nathan Foote[8], Dr. Thomas Foote[7], John Foote[6], Robert Foote[5], Nathaniel Foote[4], Sir Robert of Shalford Foote[3], Robert (John) Foote[2], John Foote[1]) was born on January 15, 1863 in Madison, New York[384] and died on June 14, 1945 in Utica, New York.[385] He married Mary Etta Clancy on December 27, 1888 in Utica, New York, the daughter of John H. Clancy and Mary Ann Donovan. She was born on August 09, 1864 in Redfield, New York[386] and died on July 11, 1923 at 1210 Churchill Avenue, Utica, New York[387]. In the 1880 Oneida Census, George was listed as Lynn Foote and lived with the Baker family. He was a member of Sacred Heart Church. The 1887 Utica Directory listed George as a moulder living at 96 Fayette Street, Utica, New York. In the 1920 Census, George was

living in Syracuse, New York on Burnet Avenue, Ward 5, with his wife, Mary, and his occupation was listed as an iron moulder. George was living with his daughter, Mary Agnes Emery, at time of his death at 1131 Downer Avenue, Utica, New York.   For more on Mary Etta Clancy see Chapter Three.

Photo of George L. Foote and Mary Clancy Foote with their daughters ,
Isabel Lydia, Mary Agnes and Edna Cecelia Foote about 1910 from the collection of Howard Hart and used with permission.

George L. Foote Jr. and Mary Etta Clancy had the following children:

31.   i.   Mary Agnes Foote was born August 16, 1890[388] in Utica, New York and died March 27, 1982 in Lakeland, Florida.[389].
32.   ii.   Isabel Lydia Foote was born January 08, 1894 [390] in Milford, Massachusetts and died August 31, 1973 in New Hartford, New York[391].

---

[384] Obituary Utica Newspaper, June 15, 1945
[385] Obituary Utica Newspaper, June 15, 1945
[386] Obituary Utica Newspaper, July 12, 1923
[387] Obituary Utica Newspaper, July 12, 1923
[388] Obituary Utica Newspaper, March 28, 1982
[389] Obituary Utica Newspaper, March 28, 1982
[390] Obituary Utica Newspaper, November 1, 1973
[391] Obituary Utica Newspaper, November 1, 1973

iii.   Edna Cecelia Foote was born January 11, 1897[392] in Utica, New York and died September 22, 1987 in Lakeland, Florida[393]. She married Edward James Hickey in June 1917 in St. Patrick's Church, Utica, New York[394]. Edna received her education in the Utica schools and worked as a postal clerk. She and Ed lived in Rome, New York, until they retired in Florida 30 years before her death. She was a member of St. Joseph's Church, Lakeland, Florida.

23. Charles Lewis Foote Jr.[11] (George L. Foote Sr.[10], Jesse Selkrigg Foote[9], Dr. Nathan Foote[8], Dr. Thomas Foote[7], John Foote[6], Robert Foote[5], Nathaniel Foote[4], Sir Robert of Shalford Foote[3], Robert (John) Foote[2], John Foote[1]) was born on January 04, 1874 in Madison, New York[395] and died on December 17, 1950 in Oneida City Hospital, Oneida, New York[396]. He married Zoola Read on January 17, 1895 in Canastota, New York, the daughter of Edward R. Read and Sarah M. Eldred. She was born on August 28, 1878 in Canastota, New York[397] and died on September 25, 1955 in Community Hospital, Hamilton, New York[398].   Charles was a foreman of the General Aniline & Film Corporation, Binghamton, New York and retired in 1944. He was a member of the Morrisville Methodist Church and of the Odd Fellows Lodge of Johnson City, New York. He had a granddaughter in 1950 by the name of Mrs. Preben Hensen of Johnson City, New York. At the turn of the century Charles conducted a laundry in the present American Legion dugout in Depot Street, Morrisville, New York.

Zoola was the president of the Madison County Women's Christian Temperance Union. She was also a Gold Star Mother, a member of the American Legion Auxiliary, the Grange, and the Methodist Church of Morrisville.

Photo of Carl, Earl and Stewart Foote in the author's collection.

---

[392] Obituary Utica Newspaper, September 23, 1987
[393] Obituary Utica Newspaper, September 23, 1987
[394] Wedding Announcement, Utica Newspaper
[395] World War I draft registration on Ancestry.com
[396] Obituary, Oneida Daily Dispatch, December 18, 1950
[397] Obituary, Oneida Daily Dispatch, September 26, 1955
[398] Obituary, Oneida Daily Dispatch, September 26, 1955

Charles Lewis Foote and Zoola Read had the following children:

i.   Harold Foote was born November 13, 1895 in Canastota, New York[399] and died November 14, 1895 in Canastota, New York[400]. Harold died as an infant and is buried with his parents. There is no date listed on the tombstone.

ii.   Carl L. Foote was born January 18, 1897[401] and died June 23, 1918 in Chateau Thierry, France[402] Carl enlisted in the United States Army to fight in World War I, June 18, 1917 at Utica, New York. He served in the Camp Syracuse branch of the 9th Infantry. He was deployed to go overseas September 6, 1917. As a Private 1st Class, he was killed in action at Chateau Thierry, France, on June 23, 1918.

33.   iii.   Earl E. Foote was born February 28, 1898[403] and died November 16, 1959.[404]

iv.   Stewart J. Foote was born March 22, 1900 in Canastota, New York[405] and died April 30, 1953 in Binghamton City Hospital, Binghamton, New York[406]. Stewart lived in Binghamton in 1950. He was a veteran of World War I. He enlisted August 28, 1917 at Utica, New York. He went to the Great Lakes Training Station in Illinois. He was a Seaman 2nd Class in the US Navy assigned to Sub Chaser 328 at Little Falls; Annapolis where 328 was used as training ship. He was discharged February 28, 1919. He had three stepchildren at the time of his death and a granddaughter.

24. Earl James Foote [11] (George L. Foote Sr.[10], Jesse Selkrigg Foote[9], Dr. Nathan Foote[8], Dr. Thomas Foote[7], John Foote[6], Robert Foote[5], Nathaniel Foote[4], Sir Robert of Shalford Foote[3], Robert (John) Foote[2], John Foote[1]) was born on March 12, 1878 in New York State[407] and died on November 20, 1971 in Canastota, New York[408]. He married Claudia C. Baker in 1900 in Hamilton, New York. She was born in 1882 in Pine Woods, New York[409] and died on April 09, 1957 in Lenox Memorial Hospital, Lenox, New York[410]. Earl lived at 401 N. Main Street, Canastota, New York at time of his death and was a member of the Canastota Methodist Church. He had worked for Niagara Mohawk for many years as a meter reader. He had three grandchildren and 8 great-grandchildren at the time of his death.

[399] Obituary, Oneida Daily Dispatch, November 15, 1895
[400] Obituary, Oneida Daily Dispatch, November 15, 1895
[401] Herkimer County, New York Soldiers at Ancestry.com
[402] Oneida Daily Dispatch Death Notice
[403] Obituary, Utica Newspaper, November 17, 1959
[404] Obituary, Utica Newspaper, November 17, 1959
[405] New York State Vital Records
[406] Obituary Canastota Newspaper, May 7, 1953
[407] World War I draft registration on Ancestry.com
[408] Obituary, Oneida Daily Dispatch, November 21, 1971
[409] Obituary, Oneida Daily Dispatch, April 10, 1957
[410] Obituary, Oneida Daily Dispatch, April 10, 1957

Earl James Foote and Claudia C. Baker had the following child:
34. i. Hazel E. Foote was born April 29, 1907 in Canastota, New York[411] and died May 29, 1995 in Oneida City Hospital, Oneida, New York[412].

Generation Twelve

Photo of a Foote Family Picnic about 1925 in the author's collection. Front Row: Zoola Foote, Harold and Gordon Emery, Billy Dolan, Howard and Hazel Hart, Hazel and Earl Foote. Second Row: Agnes Foote Emery, Art Light, Charles Dolan and Laura Rudd Dolan, Isabel Foote Light, George Foote, Edna Foote Hickey, Charles Foote and Fred Emery

---

[411] Obituary, Oneida Daily Dispatch, May 30, 1995
[412] Obituary, Oneida Daily Dispatch, May 30, 1995

25. Charles Jacob Foote [12] (Hiram Foote[11], Hiram Foote [10], Jesse Selkrigg Foote[9], Dr. Nathan Foote[8], Dr. Thomas Foote[7], John Foote[6], Robert Foote[5], Nathaniel Foote[4], Sir Robert of Shalford Foote[3], Robert (John) Foote[2], John Foote[1]) was born in 1864 in New York State[413] and died in August 30, 1904[414]. He married a girl by the name of Edith Annie McDougall, about 1895, who was born in September 1866 in England[415]. Charles was a well known musician and a member of the Grand Opera House Orchestra. He had a wife and three children at the time of his death. Edith was listed in the 1910 Syracuse Census, Ward 1, as living with her in-laws. She was a widow and worked in as dresser in a theatre.

Photos of Charles Jacob Foote and Edith Annie McDougall from the collection of Mary Hill and used with permission.

Charles Jacob Foote and Edith Annie McDougall had the following children:

35.   i.   Julia Foote was born August 10, 1896 in New York State[416] and died in August 1985[417].

36.   ii.   Catherine Edith Foote was born in November 3, 1898 in New York State[418] and died November 10, 1963[419].

---

[413] 1870 Syracuse, New York Census
[414] Death notice, Syracuse Telegram, August 31, 1904
[415] 1900 Syracuse, New York Census
[416] Social Security Death Index at Ancestry.com
[417] Social Security Death Index at Ancestry.com
[418] E-mail from Mary Ingram Hill daughter Catherine Edith Foote Ingram 4/14/10
[419] E-mail from Mary Ingram Hill daughter Catherine Edith Foote Ingram 4/14/10

iii.   Mary Dorothy Foote was born in November 1, 1902 in Syracuse, New York[420] and died July 29, 1927 in Syracuse, New York[421]. Mary Dorothy was never married.

Photo of Mary Dorothy Foote taken in 1920 from the collection of Mary Ingram Hill and used with permission.

26. Coleman M. Foote [12] (Milton Mason Foote[11], Joseph Hosley Foote [10], Jesse Selkrigg Foote[9], Dr. Nathan Foote[8], Dr. Thomas Foote[7], John Foote[6], Robert Foote[5], Nathaniel Foote[4], Sir Robert of Shalford Foote[3], Robert (John) Foote[2], John Foote[1]) was born in February 1868 in New York State[422]. He married a girl by the name of Etta N. in 1898[423]. She was born in August 1874 in New York State[424]. Coleman lived in Syracuse in the 1910 Census, but his wife was alone in the 1920 Syracuse Census. He was back in the 1930 Syracuse Census.

Coleman M. Foote and Etta N. had the following children:
37.   i.   Lucius Coman Foote was born August 27, 1899 in New York State[425] and died October 05, 1984 in Crouse Irving Memorial Hospital, Syracuse, New York[426].
    ii.   Elizabeth I. Foote was born 1912 in New York State[427].

27. Elmer Mason Foote [12] (Milton M. Foote[11], Joseph Hosley Foote [10], Jesse Selkrigg Foote[9], Dr. Nathan Foote[8], Dr. Thomas Foote[7], John Foote[6], Robert Foote[5], Nathaniel Foote[4] Nathaniel Foote[4], Sir Robert of Shalford Foote[3], Robert (John) Foote[2], John Foote[1]) was born on April 08, 1886 in Syracuse, New York[428] and died on July 16, 1973 in Community Memorial Hospital, Hamilton, New York[429]. He married a girl by the name of Blanche Isabelle Lydia in 1909[430]. She was born on December 06, 1887 in New York State[431] and died in February 1984 in Madison, New York. Elmer was a former

[420] E-mail from Mary Ingram Hill daughter Catherine Edith Foote Ingram 4/14/10
[421] E-mail from Mary Ingram Hill daughter Catherine Edith Foote Ingram 4/14/10
[422] 1900 Syracuse, New York Census
[423] 1900 Syracuse, New York Census
[424] 1900 Syracuse, New York Census
[425] World War I draft registration on Ancestry.com
[426] Obituary, Syracuse Newspaper, October 7, 1984
[427] 1930 Syracuse, New York Census
[428] World War I draft registration on Ancestry.com
[429] Obituary, Syracuse Newspaper, July 16, 1973
[430] 1930 Ithaca, New York Census
[431] Social Security Death Index at Ancestry.com

resident of Elmira and Ithaca. He had been a printer for 55 years. He was a member of the Cooley Masonic Lodge of Elmira, American Pressman Union of Elmira, and the Lowman Methodist Church, Lowman, New York.

Elmer Mason Foote and Blanche Isabelle Lydia had the following children:
i.   Frederick F. Foote was born in 1913 in New York State[432]. Frederick lived in Alexandria, Virginia in 1973.
ii.   Elmer Eugene Foote was born March 29, 1925 in New York State[433]. Elmer lived in Jamesville, New York in 1973.

28. Mildred E. Foote[12] (William H. Foote[11], George L. Foote, Sr. [10], Jesse Selkrigg Foote[9], Dr. Nathan Foote[8], Dr. Thomas Foote[7], John Foote[6], Robert Foote[5], Nathaniel Foote[4] Nathaniel Foote[4], Sir Robert of Shalford Foote[3], Robert (John) Foote[2], John Foote[1]) was born on June 10, 1884[434] and died December 19, 1964 in Utica, New York[435]. She married Maurice J. O'Connell on June 18, 1901 in Utica, New York[436]. He was born on February 18, 1876[437]. Mildred lived in Cortland in 1938.

Children of Mildred E. Foote and Maurice J. O'Connell had the following children:
38. i.   Helene L. O'Connell was born April 04, 1902 in Cortland, New York[438] and died May 08, 1986 in Rome Hospital, Rome, New York[439].
39. ii.   Robert Daniel O'Connell was born September 01, 1910 in Cortland, New York[440] and died June 22, 1998 in Bloomfield, Connecticut[441].

29. Anna Lydia Mather[12] (Mary Abigale Foote[11], George L. Foote, Sr. [10], Jesse Selkrigg Foote[9], Dr. Nathan Foote[8], Dr. Thomas Foote[7], John Foote[6], Robert Foote[5], Nathaniel Foote[4], Sir Robert of Shalford Foote[3], Robert (John) Foote[2], John Foote[1]) was born on April 26, 1875 in Madison, New York[442] and died on March 15, 1969 at 9 West Street, Whitesboro, New York[443]. She married Frank W. Rudd in 1896 in Utica, New York[444].

[432] 1930 Ithaca, New York Census
[433] Birthdatabase.com
[434] Foote Family History and Genealogy, Volume One by Abram W. Foote, page 446
[435] Obituary, Utica Newspaper, December 21, 1964
[436] Foote Family History and Genealogy, Volume One by Abram W. Foote, page 446
[437] World War I draft registration on Ancestry.com
[438] Obituary, Rome Newspaper, May 9, 1986
[439] Obituary, Rome Newspaper, May 9, 1986
[440] Obituary, The Hartford Journal, June 24, 1998
[441] Obituary, The Hartford Journal, June 24, 1998
[442] Obituary Utica Newspaper, March 16, 1969
[443] Obituary Utica Newspaper, March 16, 1969
[444] 1900 Town of Lenox, Madison County, New York Census

He was born in July 1873 in New York State[445] and died on October 17, 1906 in Greenway, New York[446]. She later married Emery C. Inman on June 17, 1910 in Mary Mather's home, Powell Avenue, Whitesboro, New York[447]. He was the son of George and Helen Inman. He was born on July 16, 1875 in Fenner, New York[448] and died on June 17, 1937 in Rome Hospital, Rome, New York[449].

In the photo of her grandfather's 90th birthday, Anna was listed as Annie in 1908 photo, which appeared in the Syracuse newspaper. She attended school in Madison, New York. She moved to Canastota at an early age. She lived with her daughter, Laura Dillon, since 1936. She was of the Protestant faith.

Photo of Anna Lydia Mather from the collection of Susan Whitman and used with permission.

Canastota Newspaper, October 21, 1905

Frank Rudd, a New York Central freight brakeman living at East Syracuse, was struck by the westbound Empire State Express at Greenway Tuesday afternoon and instantly killed. Engineman George Gilbert of the Empire saw the man sitting on the rail of Track No. 2 upon which the Empire was approaching. Gilbert sounded the whistle several times. He noticed that the man did not leave the track. Before he could stop his engine the unfortunate man had been thrown high in the air, his skull crushed and the head nearly severed from the body. It was said that Rudd was on his way to flag for a stalled freight train and he had fallen asleep sitting on the track. Upon instruction from New York City the engine and caboose of Rudd's train conveyed the body to East Syracuse. Undertaker Andrew Behr, of East Syracuse, went to Greenway and accompanied the remains home.

Frank lived with the Gleason family in the 1880 Census in Lenox, New York. He was 12 years old at the time.

---

[445] 1900 Town of Lenox, Madison County, New York Census
[446] Obituary, Canastota Newspaper, October 18, 1906
[447] Wedding Announcement, Utica Newspaper
[448] Obituary, Rome Sentinel, June 18, 1937
[449] Social Security Death Index at Ancestry.com

Anna Lydia Mather and Frank W. Rudd had the following child:

40.   i.   Laura (Iva) Rudd was born February 18, 1898 in New York State[450] and died December 30, 1993 in Rome, New York[451].

Photo of Anna Lydia Mather, Laura Rudd and Frank W. Rudd from the collection of Susan Whitman and used with permission.

Anna Lydia Mather and Emery C. Inman had the following child:

   i.   Ruth Helen Inman was born July 29, 1912 in Whitesboro, New York[452] and died August 08, 1936 in St. Luke's Hospital, Utica, New York[453]. Ruth committed suicide by taking poison. She took the poison Friday night and died the next day in the hospital. Ruth has resided in Whitesboro until two before her death, when she moved with her family to Utica. She had been employed by J. B. Wells & Son Company store for six years, having been assigned to the receiving room. She attended the Methodist Church and was a member of the Queen Esther Society of the Methodist Church of Whitesboro, New York.

30. Gertrude M. Mather[12] (Mary Abigale Foote[11], George L. Foote, Sr. [10], Jesse Selkrigg Foote[9], Dr. Nathan Foote[8], Dr. Thomas Foote[7], John Foote[6], Robert Foote[5], Nathaniel Foote[4], Sir Robert of Shalford Foote[3], Robert (John) Foote[2], John Foote[1]) was born on April 09, 1876 in Siloam, New York[454] and died on May 06, 1963 in St. Luke's Memorial Hospital, New Hartford, New York[455]. She married Dayton R. Mallette in 1912. He was born in 1853 in New York State[456] and was from Canajoharie. She later married George Moore. He died in 1958[457]. He was from East Worcester. Gertrude lived in Whitesboro in 1913 and at 1 Powell Avenue in Whitesboro in 1914. The 1910 Census for Whitestown said she was a buttonholer in the knitting mills. Gertrude was educated in Canastota Schools and later moved to Whitesboro where she had been employed by the

---

[450] Obituary, Rome Sentinel, December 31, 1993
[451] Obituary, Rome Sentinel, December 31, 1993
[452] Obituary Utica Newspaper, August 9, 1936
[453] Obituary Utica Newspaper, August 9, 1936
[454] Foote Family History and Genealogy, Volume One by Abram W. Foote
[455] Obituary Utica Newspaper, May 7, 1963
[456] 1920 Rome, New York Census
[457] Obituary of wife, Utica Newspaper, May 7, 1963

Alliance Knitting Mill. For five years prior to her death, she had lived with her niece, Mrs. Laura Dillon. Gertrude was of the Baptist faith.

Gertrude M. Mather and Dayton R. Mallette had the following child:

41.   i.   Lee J. Mallette was born March 02, 1916 in New York State[458] and died November 23, 1999 in Hemet, California[459].

Photo of Gertrude M. Mather Mallette Moore and her mother Anna Foote Mather from the collection of Susan Whitman and used with permission.

31. Mary Agnes Foote[12] (George L. Foote Sr.[11], George L. Foote Sr.[10], Jesse Selkrigg Foote[9], Dr. Nathan Foote[8], Dr. Thomas Foote[7], John Foote[6], Robert Foote[5], Nathaniel Foote[4], Sir Robert of Shalford Foote[3], Robert (John) Foote[2], John Foote[1]) was born on August 16, 1890[460] in Utica, New York and died on March 27, 1982 in Lakeland, Florida[461]. She married Alcide F. Emery on July 14, 1909 in St. Patrick's Church, Utica, New York[462], the son of Jean (John) Baptist Emery and Celina Gagnier. He was born on May 18, 1885 in Stoney Point, Ontario, Canada[463] and died on July 12, 1961 in Utica, New York.[464]   For more on Alcide Emery, see Chapter One.

Photo of Mary Agnes Foote, age 19, and Alcide Emery, age 24, from the author's collection.

[458] Social Security Death Index at Ancestry.com
[459] Social Security Death Index at Ancestry.com
[460] Obituary Utica Newspaper, March 28, 1982
[461] Obituary Utica Newspaper, March 28, 1982
[462] Wedding Announcement, Utica Newspaper
[463] Naturalization papers
[464] Obituary Utica Newspaper, July 13, 1961

Mary Agnes Foote and Alcide F. Emery had the following children:

42.   i.   Harold Alcide Emery was born July 21, 1913 in Utica, New York[465] and died December 11, 1989 in New Hartford, New York.[466].

43.   ii.   Gordon Charles Emery was born March 29, 1915 in Utica, New York[467] and died October 09, 1981 in Utica, New York.[468]

32. Isabel Lydia Foote[12] (George L. Foote Sr.[11], George L. Foote Sr.[10], Jesse Selkrigg Foote[9], Dr. Nathan Foote[8], Dr. Thomas Foote[7], John Foote[6], Robert Foote[5], Nathaniel Foote[4], Sir Robert of Shalford Foote[3], Robert (John) Foote[2], John Foote[1]) was born on January 08, 1894 in Milford, Massachusetts[469] and died on August 31, 1973 in New Hartford, New York[470]. She married Bert Raynor Hart in 1911 in Morrisville, New York. He was born in November 06, 1885[471] in New York State[472] and died on February 23, 1927[473].   Following her marriage to Bert, she married Arthur Light. Later she married

Claude L. Earley in 1941 in Massena, New York[474], the son of Fred G. Earley and Lizzie M. Hugill. He was born on May 04, 1904 in Vernon Center, New York[475] and died on April 16, 1986 in the Sitrin Nursing Home, New Hartford, New York[476]. Isabel was listed as the legal guardian for her children the will of Bert Raynor Hart. Isabel lived at 2218 Highland Ave. at time of her death. She was a member of Sacred Heart Church. Claude was a graduate of Westmoreland High School. He was a self employed electrician in the Utica area for many years. He was of the Methodist Faith.

Photo of Isabel Lydia Foote taken in Worcester, Massachusetts in the author's collection.

[465] Obituary Utica Newspaper, December 12, 1989
[466] Obituary Utica Newspaper, December 12, 1989
[467] Social Security Death Index at Ancestry.com
[468] Death Certificate
[469] Obituary Utica Newspaper, September 1, 1973
[470] Obituary Utica Newspaper, September 1, 1973
[471] World War I Draft Registration at Ancestry.com
[472] 1920 Rome, New York Census
[473] Will of Burt R. Hart
[474] Ancestry.com, One World Tree
[475] Obituary Utica Newspaper, April 17, 1986
[476] Obituary Utica Newspaper, April 17, 1986

Photo of Claude Earley, Isabel Foote Hart Earley, Howard Hart Jr., Kathleen, Nancy and Robert Collins from the collection of Howard Hart Jr. and used with permission.

Isabel Lydia Foote and Bert Raynor Hart had the following children:

44. i. Hazel Hart was born May 10, 1912 in Morrisville, New York[477] and died July 10, 1949 in Memorial Hospital, Utica, New York[478].

45. ii. Howard John Hart was born September 16, 1914 in Eaton, New York[479] and died February 25, 1990 in St. Elizabeth Hospital, Utica, New York[480].

33. Earl E. Foote[12] (Charles Lewis Foote[11], George L. Foote Sr.[10], Jesse Selkrigg Foote[9], Dr. Nathan Foote[8], Dr. Thomas Foote[7], John Foote[6], Robert Foote[5], Nathaniel Foote[4], Sir Robert of Shalford Foote[3], Robert (John) Foote[2], John Foote[1]) was born on January 18, 1898[481] and died November 16, 1959[482]. Earl was found dead at his home and had been dead about two days. He was an employee of Henney Motors Co. He was a veteran of World War I and a member of the Munnsville American Legion Post. He enlisted September 16th in the Ft. Slocum, Taylor branch of service, 5th infantry. He was discharged November 1919. He had three grandchildren at the time of his death. Earl married a woman by the name of Hazel who was born in 1898 and died January 24, 1963[483]. Hazel lived at 224 Harrison Street, Johnson City, New York at the time of her death. She was a member of the Primitive Methodist Church and the Sunshine Scatters Class of Sunday School. She was a retired employee of Ansco having worked for over 40 years.

Brookville Courier, October 26, 1921
Earl E Foote, 23, a former resident of Canastota was arrested in Louisville, Kentucky, charged with stealing $9,000 in two packages from the Binghamton post office where he had been employed for the past two years. He still had $5,740 left.

Earl E. Foote and Hazel had the following child:

i. Sarah E. Foote was born April 17, 1921 in New York State and died December 25, 1987 in Clallam Bay, Washington[484]. She married Preben M. Hansen. He

---

[477] Obituary Utica Newspaper, July 11, 1949
[478] Obituary Utica Newspaper, July 11, 1949
[479] Obituary Utica Newspaper, February 26, 1990
[480] Obituary Utica Newspaper, February 26, 1990
[481] Obituary Utica Newspaper, February 17, 1959
[482] Obituary Utica Newspaper, February 17, 1959
[483] Obituary, Binghamton, New York Newspaper, January 25, 1963
[484] Social Security Death Index at Ancestry.com

was born January 11, 1919[485] and died July 20, 1998 in Suquamish, Kitsap, Washington[486].

34. Hazel E. Foote[12] (Earl James Foote[11], George L. Foote Sr.[10], Jesse Selkrigg Foote[9], Dr. Nathan Foote[8], Dr. Thomas Foote[7], John Foote[6], Robert Foote[5], Nathaniel Foote[4], Sir Robert of Shalford Foote[3], Robert (John) Foote[2], John Foote[1]) was born on April 29, 1907 in Canastota, New York[487] and died on May 29, 1995 in Oneida City Hospital, Oneida, New York[488]. She married Raymond A. Rousseau on April 25, 1926 in New Hartford, New York.

He was born in 1904[489] and died on December 31, 1956[490]. Hazel lived in the Canastota area most of her life, moving to Oneida in 1972. She was a bookkeeper at the former Avon Theater in Canastota for more than twenty years, retiring in 1952. She was a Protestant.

Hazel E. Foote and Raymond A. Rousseau had the following children:

    i.   Living Rousseau
    ii.   Living Rousseau

46.   iii.   Richard C. Rousseau was born September 30, 1928 in Canastota, New York [491] and died October 21, 1999 in Stonehedge Health and Rehabilitation Center, Chittenango, New York.

Generation Thirteen

35. Julia Foote[13] (Charles Foote [12], Hiram Foote[11], Hiram Foote [10], Jesse Selkrigg Foote[9], Dr. Nathan Foote[8], Dr. Thomas Foote[7], John Foote[6], Robert Foote[5], Nathaniel Foote[4], Sir Robert of Shalford Foote[3], Robert (John) Foote[2], John Foote[1]) was born August 10, 1896 in New York State [492] and died in August 29, 1985[493]. She married James Whitehead on December 25, 1916 at the home of her mother[494]. He was born October 12, 1891 in England[495] and died in April 1975 in Syracuse, New York.[496] Julia was a lifelong

---

[485] Social Security Death Index at Ancestry.com
[486] Social Security Death Index at Ancestry.com
[487] Obituary, Oneida Newspaper, May 30, 1995
[488] Obituary, Oneida Newspaper, May 30, 1995
[489] Mt. Pleasant Cemetery, Canastota, New York
[490] Obituary of wife, Oneida Newspaper, May 30, 1995
[491] Obituary, Rome Sentinel, October 22, 1999
[492] Family information form Mary Ingram Hill
[493] Obituary, Syracuse Herald Journal, August 20, 1895
[494] Wedding Announcement, Syracuse New York Daily Journal, December 26, 1916
[495] World War I draft registration on Ancestry.com
[496] Social Security Death Index at Ancestry.com

resident of Syracuse, New York. She was a member of Gethsamane united Methodist Church. James came to America in 1906 from Manchester, England and lived in Syracuse, New York the rest of his life. He was a 50 year member of the Oddfellows, a past noble grand knight, a district deputy and a member of the Order of the Orientals. He also was a member of the Quarter century Club of Crouse Hinds Company, Dad's Club of Foreign Service Veterans Mattydale Post 239 and Gethsemane United Methodist Church.

Photo of Julia, James and Charles Whitehead taken in 1919 from the collection of Mary Ingram Hill and used with permission.

Julia Foote and James Whitehead had the following children:

i.   Living Whitehead

ii.   James Whitehead was born on September 13, 1921 in Syracuse, New York and died on October 04, 2002 in Syracuse, New York[497]. James retired in 1985 as a foreman in the non-ferrous foundry at Crouse Hinds Company in Syracuse, New York, after 47 years of service. He was a member of Gethsemane United Methodist Church in Syracuse, the American Legion Post 1832 in Mattydale, and Salina Senior Citizens of Liverpool, New York. He was a life member of the Pastime Athletic Club and was an Army Air Force veteran of World War II. James was married and had one child who may still be living.

iii.   Robert F. Whitehead was born March 19, 1923[498] in Syracuse, New York and died August 20, 2001 in Syracuse, New York[499]. Robert retired from Crouse Hinds Company after 45 years and was a member of its retirees group and Quarter century Club. He was a live member of Pastime Athletic Club, a member of Saline Senior Citizens and Mattydale VFW Post. He was an Army veteran of World War II. Robert was married and he and his wife had two children who may still be living.

iv.   Norman T. Whitehead was born July 31, 1925 in Syracuse, New York[500] and died September 22, 2000 in Syracuse, New York[501]. Norman married Virginia L. Baker, the daughter of Harry and Kathleen Baker[502]. She was born May 30, 1924 in Syracuse, New York[503] and died January 28, 2009 at Rosewood Heights Nursing Home[504]. Norman retired in 1988 after 42 years as a bench filer at Crouse Hinds Company. He was a member of the International Brotherhood of Electrical Workers

---

[497] Obituary, Syracuse Post Standard, October 5, 2002
[498] Bible pages from the bible of Julia Foote Whitehead
[499] Obituary, Syracuse Newspaper, August 21, 2001
[500] Bible pages from the bible of Julia Foote Whitehead
[501] Obituary, Syracuse Herald Journal Newspaper, September 24, 2000
[502] Obituary, Syracuse Post Standard Newspaper, February 1, 2009
[503] Social Security Death Index at Ancestry.com
[504] Obituary, Syracuse Post Standard Newspaper, February 1, 2009

Local 2084, the Gethsemane United Methodist Church and the Mattydale Senior Citizens. He was a life member and captain of the fire police of the Mattydale Volunteer Fire Department and a life member and past commander of Mattydale Veterans of Foreign Wars Post 3146. Virginia worked as an assembler at Crouse Hinds Company was former member of MVFD Ladies Auxiliary, VFW Ladies Auxiliary Post #3146 in Mattydale and the Mattydale-Hinsdale Senior Citizens. He was also a member of the Gethsemane United Methodist Church. Norman T Whitehead and Virginia L. Baker had three children who may still be living.

     v.   Billy Whitehead was born October 17, 1927 and died October 19, 1927[505].

     vi.   Living Whitehead

36.   Catherine Edith Foote[13] (Charles Foote [12], Hiram Foote[11], Hiram Foote [10], Jesse Selkrigg Foote[9], Dr. Nathan Foote[8], Dr. Thomas Foote[7], John Foote[6], Robert Foote[5], Nathaniel Foote[4], Sir Robert of Shalford Foote[3], Robert (John) Foote[2], John Foote[1]) was born November 3, 1898 in Syracuse, New York[506] and died August 23, 1930 in Syracuse,

New York[507]. Catherine married Alfred Harold Ingram on August 13, 1930 in Syracuse, New York[508]. He was born on January 27, 1896 in Wolverhampton, Staffordshire, England[509] and he died April 30, 1937 in Salina, Onondaga County, New York[510].

Photo of Catherine Edith Foote from the collection of Mary Ingram Hill and used with permission.

Catherine Edith Foote and Alfred Harold Ingram had the following children:

     i.   Harold H. Ingram was born March 21, 1921[511] and died January 23, 2010 in Tucson, Arizona[512]. He married Margaret Marie Rannow on October 13, 1945 in Tempe, Arizona[513].

     ii.   June Marie Ingram was born June 8, 1922[514] and died May 1, 1995 in Salem, Oregon[515]. She married Russell Emil Henry Bieraugel on August 2, 1940 in Washington, D.C.[516]

[505] Bible pages from the bible of Julia Foote Whitehead
[506] E-mail from Mary Ingram Hill daughter Catherine Edith Foote Ingram 4/14/10
[507] E-mail from Mary Ingram Hill daughter Catherine Edith Foote Ingram 4/14/10
[508] Family information from Mary Ingram Hill daughter of Catherine Edith Foote Ingram
[509] Family information from Mary Ingram Hill daughter of Catherine Edith Foote Ingram
[510] Family information from Mary Ingram Hill daughter of Catherine Edith Foote Ingram
[511] Social Security Index at Ancestry.com
[512] Family information from Mary Ingram Hill daughter of Catherine Edith Foote Ingram
[513] Family information from Mary Ingram Hill daughter of Catherine Edith Foote Ingram

iii.   Ronald D. Ingram was born January 10, 1924 in Syracuse, New York[517] and died December 1, 2007 in Los Angeles, California[518]. He did not marry.

iv.   Patricia Ann Ingram was born August 17, 1930 in Syracuse, New York[519] and died July 18, 1999 in Cody Park, Wyoming[520], She married Jay Welch Brown on May 31, 1961 in Salt Lake City, Utah[521].

v.   Mary Dorothy Ingram was born in the Town of Camillus, Onondaga, New York. She married Donald Ramon Hill on August 29, 1952 in Sand Diego, California[522].

vi.   Wilma Sue Ingram was born June 25, 1933 in Syracuse, New York[523] and died December 15, 1998 in Detroit, Michigan[524]. She married Bobby Jack Thompson on June 16, 1959 in San Diego, California[525].

vii.   David Leighton Ingram was born December 8, 1935 in Syracuse, New York[526] and died October 5, 1983 in Cazenovia, New York[527]. He married Beatrice Fanny Coon on March 23, 1957[528].

37. Lucius Coman Foote[13] (Coleman M. Foote[12], Milton Mason Foote[11], Joseph Hosley Foote [10], Jesse Selkrigg Foote[9], Dr. Nathan Foote[8], Dr. Thomas Foote[7], John Foote[6], Robert Foote[5], Nathaniel Foote[4], Sir Robert of Shalford Foote[3], Robert (John) Foote[2], John Foote[1]) was born on August 27, 1899 in New York State[529] and died on October 05, 1984 in Crouse Irving Memorial Hospital, Syracuse, New York[530]. He married a lady by the name of Dr. Catherine K. Lucius and was a life resident of Syracuse. He was a 1922 graduate of Syracuse University College of Engineering and was a self employed manufacturer representative and the owner of L.C. Foote & Associates. He was a member of DeWitt Community Church, the Syracuse Community Orchestra and the Upstate Representativeness Association. Lucius was an avid outdoors man and a member of the

[514] Julia Foote Whitehead bible pages
[515] Family information from Mary Ingram Hill daughter of Catherine Edith Foote Ingram
[516] Family information from Mary Ingram Hill daughter of Catherine Edith Foote Ingram
[517] Julia Foote Whitehead bible pages
[518] Family information from Mary Ingram Hill daughter of Catherine Edith Foote Ingram
[519] Julia Foote Whitehead bible pages
[520] Family information from Mary Ingram Hill daughter of Catherine Edith Foote Ingram
[521] Family information from Mary Ingram Hill daughter of Catherine Edith Foote Ingram
[522] Family information from Mary Ingram Hill daughter of Catherine Edith Foote Ingram
[523] Julia Foote Whitehead bible pages
[524] Family information from Mary Ingram Hill daughter of Catherine Edith Foote Ingram
[525] Family information from Mary Ingram Hill daughter of Catherine Edith Foote Ingram
[526] Family information from Mary Ingram Hill daughter of Catherine Edith Foote Ingram
[527] Family information from Mary Ingram Hill daughter of Catherine Edith Foote Ingram
[528] Family information from Mary Ingram Hill daughter of Catherine Edith Foote Ingram
[529] World War I draft registration on Ancestry.com
[530] Obituary, Syracuse Newspaper, October 6, 1984

Adirondack Mountain Club and had climbed many of the high peaks of the Adirondacks. He was an Army veteran of World War I. Lucius Coman Foote and Dr. Catherine K. Lucius had three children who may still be living.

38. Helene L. O'Connell[13] (Mildred E. Foote[12], William H. Foote[11], George L. Foote Sr.[10], Jesse Selkrigg Foote[9], Dr. Nathan Foote[8], Dr. Thomas Foote[7], John Foote[6], Robert Foote[5], Nathaniel Foote[4], Sir Robert of Shalford Foote[3], Robert (John) Foote[2], John Foote[1]) was born on April 04, 1902 in Cortland, New York[531] and died on May 08, 1986 in Rome Hospital, Rome, New York[532]. She married James M. O'Hara on August 14, 1930 in Cortland, New York, the son of Michael and Margaret O'Hara. He was born in 1901 in Turin, Lewis County, New York[533] and died on December 28, 1955 in Syracuse, New York[534]. Helene had lived in Rome since 1924. She was a member of St. Peter's Church, the Syracuse University Alumni Association, Theta Phi Alpha Sorority and Phi Beta Kappa National Honor Society. She had three grandchildren at the time of her death. James attended Turin High School and graduated from Utica Free Academy. He was a graduate of Syracuse University and Fordham Law School, New York City. He was associated for a time at White Plains in practice with the former Judge Humphrey J. Lynch. He opened his Utica law office in 1929 and five years later established a Rome office. From 1932 through 1934 he was sheriff's attorney under the late Albert E. Ellinger and began his term as corporation counsel in 1935. He was a member of the Knights of Columbus, the Elks and belonged to St. Peter's Church. Helene L. O'Connell and James M. O'Hara had one child who may still be living.

39. Robert Daniel O'Connell[13] (Mildred E. Foote[12], William H. Foote[11], George L. Foote Sr.[10], Jesse Selkrigg Foote[9], Dr. Nathan Foote[8], Dr. Thomas Foote[7], John Foote[6], Robert Foote[5], Nathaniel Foote[4], Sir Robert of Shalford Foote[3], Robert (John) Foote[2], John Foote[1]) was born on September 01, 1910 in Cortland, New York[535] and died on June 22, 1998 in Bloomfield, Connecticut[536]. He married Maree Basttista on June 05, 1937. Robert was a four letter man in high school. He played football under Knute Rockne at Notre Dame. After transferring to Yale in his sophomore year, he played varsity football and basketball, including one season with Albie Booth as captain. He also captained a championship basketball team at Yale in 1932/33. After graduating Yale, he entered

[531] Obituary, Rome Sentinel, May 9, 1986
[532] Obituary, Rome Sentinel, May 9, 1986
[533] Obituary, Rome Sentinel, December 29, 1955
[534] Obituary, Rome Sentinel, December 29, 1955
[535] Obituary, The Hartford Journal, Hartford, Connecticut, June 24, 1998
[536] Obituary, The Hartford Journal, Hartford, Connecticut, June 24, 1998

Yale Law School and graduated in 1936. His career was in insurance, having worked at the Traveler's Company and the Aetna Insurance Company. Following his retirement in 1975, he worked as a consultant in Stamford and then New York City until 1984. Mr. O'Connell served for four and a half years in the U.S. Army during World War II, including one and a half years in India with the rank of Captain, working in a Branch of Intelligence. Robert Daniel O'Connell and Maree Basttista had four children who may still be living.

40. Laura (Iva) Rudd[13] (Anna Lydia Mather[12], Mary Abigale Foote[11], George L. Foote Sr[10], Jesse Selkrigg Foote[9], Dr. Nathan Foote[8], Dr. Thomas Foote[7], John Foote[6], Robert Foote[5], Nathaniel Foote[4], Sir Robert of Shalford Foote[3], Robert (John) Foote[2], John Foote[1]) was born on February 18, 1898 in New York State[537] and died on December 30, 1993 in Rome, New York[538]. She married Charles Frederick Dolan in 1916. He was born on December 03, 1891 in Cortland, New York[539] and died in 1936[540]. She later married John J. Dillon in 1937 in Scranton, Pennsylvania. John was born August 29, 1891 in Utica, New York[541] died August 12, 1952 in St. Elizabeth Hospital, Utica, New York[542].

Photo of Laura Rudd from the collection of Kerry Cannon and used with permission.

Laura had been employed for 35 years by the Boston Store. She was a member of St. Paul's Church, Whitesboro, New York. She had lived in the Colonial Apartments in Rome in her later years and then at the Stonehedge Nursing Home in Rome, New York. Laura had three great granddaughters at the time of her death and seven great-great grandchildren. The World War I draft registration indicated Charles Frederick Dolan worked as a clerk for Hart and Crouse of Utica.   John J. Dillon was educated in Utica Schools. For many years he was a salesman for the Adrean Lee Packing company. He later operated The Barn in North Utica and at the time of his death

[537] Social Security Death Index at Ancestry.com
[538] Obituary, Rome Sentinel, December 31, 1993
[539] World War I draft registration on Ancestry.com
[540] Obituary of wife, Rome Sentinel, December 31, 1993
[541] Obituary, Utica, New York Newspaper, August 13, 1952
[542] Obituary, Utica, New York Newspaper, August 13, 1952

he was a salesman for the Cudahy Packing Company in Utica, New York. He was a member of St. Peter's Church in North Utica.

Laura (Iva) Rudd and Charles Frederick Dolan had the following child:

      i.   William F. Dolan was born August 13, 1917 in Whitesboro, New York[543] and died April 19, 1997 in Rome Memorial Hospital, Rome, New York[544]. He married Eleanor King on June 15, 1940 in St. Francis Church, Utica, New York. William was educated in Utica Free Academy and St. Francis DeSales Schools and was a veteran of the U.S. Army Air Corps being stationed at Fort Slocum in 1936. He had was employed at Griffiss Air Force Base for 30 years in Civil Engineering retiring in 1969. He also drove a school bus for Birnie Bus Company for 28 years, retiring in 1996. He was a

communicant of St. Paul's Church, a life member of Knights of Columbus #391 Rome Council, a member of Friendly Sons of St. Patrick, and was an avid basketball player in the former Rome Industrial League.

Photo of William F. Dolan and Eleanor King on their wedding day June 15, 1940 from the collection of Susan Whitman and used with permission.

41. Lee J. Mallette[13] (Gertrude M. Mather[12], Mary Abigale Foote[11], George L. Foote Sr.[10], Jesse Selkrigg Foote[9], Dr. Nathan Foote[8], Dr. Thomas Foote[7], John Foote[6], Robert Foote[5], Nathaniel Foote[4], Sir Robert of Shalford Foote[3], Robert (John) Foote[2], John Foote[1]) was born on March 02, 1916 in New York State[545] and died on November 23, 1999 in Hemet, California[546]. He married a lady by the name of Alida. Lee lived at 447 E. Madison Avenue, El Cajon, California in 1963. Lee J. Mallette and Alida had three children who may still be living.

[543] Obituary, Rome Sentinel, April 20, 1997
[544] Obituary, Rome Sentinel, April 20, 1997
[545] Social Security Death Index at Ancestry.com
[546] Social Security Death Index at Ancestry.com

42. Harold Alcide Emery[13] (Mary Agnes Foote[12] , George L. Foote Jr.[11], George L. Foote Sr.[10], Jesse Selkrigg Foote[9], Dr. Nathan Foote[8], Dr. Thomas Foote[7], John Foote[6], Robert Foote[5], Nathaniel Foote[4], Sir Robert of Shalford Foote[3], Robert (John) Foote[2], John Foote[1]) was born on July 21, 1913 in Utica, New York and died on December 11, 1989 in New Hartford, New York. For more information on Harold, see Chapter One.

Photo of Harold Alcide Emery taken about 1920 in the author's collection.

43. Gordon Charles Emery[13] (Mary Agnes Foote[12] , George L Foote Jr.[11], George L. Foote Sr.[10], Jesse Selkrigg Foote[9], Dr. Nathan Foote[8], Dr. Thomas Foote[7], John Foote[6], Robert Foote[5], Nathaniel Foote[4], Sir Robert of Shalford Foote[3], Robert (John) Foote[2], John Foote[1]) was born on March 29, 1915 in Utica, New York[547] and died on October 09, 1981 in Utica, New York.[548] For more on Gordon, see Chapter One.

Photo of Gordon Charles Emery taken about 1922 and in the author's collection.

---

[547] Social Security Death Index at Ancestry.com
[548] Death Certificate

44. Hazel Hart[13] (Isabel Lydia Foote[12], George L Foote Jr.[11], George L. Foote Sr.[10], Jesse Selkrigg Foote[9], Dr. Nathan Foote[8], Dr. Thomas Foote[7], John Foote[6], Robert Foote[5], Nathaniel Foote[4], Sir Robert of Shalford Foote[3], Robert (John) Foote[2], John Foote[1]) was born on May 10, 1912 in Morrisville, New York[549] and died on July 10, 1949 in Memorial Hospital, Utica, New York[550]. She married Ivan Jay Collins on April 29, 1932. He was born in 1905 in Norwood, New York[551] and died on March 03, 1964 at 1138 Conkling Avenue, Utica, New York[552]. Hazel moved to Utica with her family in 1919 and attended local schools graduating from Utica Free Academy in 1930. She was a member of Calvary Episcopal Church and its Circle L. Ivan was a Linotype operator for the Utica Observer Dispatch for 40 years. He attended school in Norwood, New York. He worked for the Ogdensburg Journal before coming to Utica. He was a member of the International Typographical Union. Hazel Hart and Ivan Jay Collins had two children who may still be living.

Photo of Hazel Hart from the author's collection.

45. Howard John Hart[13] (Isabel Lydia Foote[12], George L Foote Jr.[11], George L. Foote Sr.[10], Jesse Selkrigg Foote[9], Dr. Nathan Foote[8], Dr. Thomas Foote[7], John Foote[6], Robert Foote[5], Nathaniel Foote[4], Sir Robert of Shalford Foote[3], Robert (John) Foote[2], John Foote[1]) was born on September 16, 1914 in Eaton, New York[553] and died on February 25, 1990 in St. Elizabeth Hospital, Utica, New York[554]. He married Elizabeth Marie Mahlmann on March 31, 1938 at the home of Rev. Walter Leo Bailey, Utica, New York,

---

[549] Obituary Utica Newspaper, July 11, 1949
[550] Obituary Utica Newspaper, July 11, 1949
[551] Obituary Utica Newspaper, March 4, 1964
[552] Obituary Utica Newspaper, March 4, 1964
[553] Obituary Utica Newspaper, February 26, 1990
[554] Obituary Utica Newspaper, February 26, 1990

the daughter of Harry C. Mahlmann and Amelia Kroutch. She was born on December 05, 1918 in Utica, New York[555] and died on October 02, 2008 in Presbyterian Home, New Hartford, New York[556]. Howard retired from the Utica Daily Press June 1, 1974 after 37 years of service on the typographical staff. He served 22 of those years as Chapel Chairman of the International Typographical Union, Local 62 Newspaper Chapel. For 35 years he operated a linotype machine. He lived at 6 Oatley Avenue, Yorkville, New York at the time of his death. He graduated from Utica Free Academy.

Photo of Howard J. Hart from the collection of Howard Hart Jr. and used with permission.

Elizabeth was also a graduate of Utica Free Academy. She worked for over 30 years for the Whitesboro School System, retiring as cafeteria manager. She was a member of the Order of Eastern Star and the Yorkville Presbyterian Church for over 50 years. She spent and enjoyed summers at Sand Bay, Clayton, New York for over 50 years at her family camp. She had seven great grandchildren at the time of her death. Howard John Hart and Elizabeth Marie Mahlmann had two children who may still be living.

46. Richard C. Rousseau[13] (Hazel E. Foote[12], Earl James Foote[11], George L. Foote Sr.[10], Jesse Selkrigg Foote[9], Dr. Nathan Foote[8], Dr. Thomas Foote[7], John Foote[6], Robert Foote[5], Nathaniel Foote[4], Sir Robert of Shalford Foote[3], Robert (John) Foote[2], John Foote[1]) was born on September 30, 1928 in Canastota, New York[557] and died on October 21, 1999 in Stonehedge Health and Rehabilitation Center, Chittenango, New York[558]. Richard spent his early years in Canastota, attending the Canastota Schools. He later lived in Verona for 28 years, moving to Florida in 1994. He spent summers at his camp in Old Forge since 1965. Richard was an avid Lionel train collector and he loved biking. He worked for the New York State Thruway Maintenance Department for 33 years, retiring in 1985. He was a member of the Loyal Order of Moose #421 of Oneida, the Verona Volunteer Fire Department, William Russell American Legion Post #404 of Vernon, and UFW Post #6811 of Verona. He was a veteran of the Korean Conflict, serving overseas with the U.S. Army. Richard had been married twice. He and his first wife had three children who may still be living.

---

[555] Obituary Utica Newspaper, October 3, 2008
[556] Obituary Utica Newspaper, October 3, 2008
[557] Obituary, Rome Sentinel, October 22, 1999
[558] Obituary, Rome Sentinel, October 22, 1999

Chapter Three

Descendants of John H. Clancy

Generation One

1. John H. Clancy[1] was born on April 22, 1834 in Ireland[1] and died on July 30, 1914 in St. Elizabeth Hospital, Utica, New York[2]. He married Mary Ann Donovan in 1855[3], the daughter of Jeremiah Donovan and Catherine Coughlin. She was born in October 1836 in Amsterdam, New York[4] and died on December 12, 1911 in St. Elizabeth Hospital, Utica, New York[5]. John and his family were living in Redfield, New York, in 1860, 1870 and 1880. John was listed as a day laborer.

In the 1870 Census, the family was still living in Redfield, New York and John was listed as a carpenter. In the 1880 Census John was listed as a farmer and was unable to read or write. In the 1900 Census, the family was living in Utica, New York. He owned his own house free of a mortgage. The census indicated he immigrated in 1854 and was listed as a laborer and a naturalized citizen.

Four generation photo of Hanna Clancy Allen, her father, John H. Clancy, her daughter, Mary Elizabeth Allen Miller and grandson, Clifford Allen Miller from the collection of Karen Skaradek and used with permission.

John died of heart disease after he had been ill for about a year. His death certificate said he died of organic disease of the heart. According to Velma Kidder, when John Clancy came to America, he landed in New York City. He first saw celery at that time and wanted to bring flowers to the people who were meeting him. He bought a bunch of celery thinking it was flowers. He went to work for the New York City Police Department as a janitor. He met his wife in New York City and they went to Oswego County, Town of Redfield to settle. John came to America 50 years ago from Ireland

---

[1] Death Certificate of John H Clancy
[2] Obituary Utica Newspaper July 31, 1914
[3] 1900 Utica New York Census, Ward 11
[4] Obituary Utica Newspaper December 13, 1911
[5] Obituary Utica Newspaper December 13, 1911

according to his obituary. He was a member of St. Patrick's Church and had lived in Utica for 29 years. The 1887-90 Utica Directory listed John living at 38 Perkins Avenue, Utica and in 1891 he was living at 256 Sunset Avenue.

Mary Ann Donovan died of diabetes and had been ill for two years prior to her death. She had eleven children; eight of them were still living in 1900. She was able to read and write. She was a member of St. Patrick's Church, Utica, New York, and the Sacred Heart Society.

Photo of Mary Ann Donovan Clancy from the author's collection.

Children of John H. Clancy and Mary Ann Donovan are:

2. i. Hannah Clancy was born February 15, 1857 in Redfield, New York[6] and died October 22, 1925 in Utica, New York[7].

ii. Jeremiah Clancy was born 1859 in New York State. Jeremiah never showed up again in any of the censuses after 1860. He must have died young.

iii. Catherine Clancy was born about 1861 in New York State[8]. She died between 1880 and 1910.

3. **iv.** **Mary Etta Clancy** was born August 09, 1864 in Redfield, New York[9], and died July 11, 1923 at 1210 Churchill Avenue, Utica, New York.[10]

4. v. Jane (Jennie) E. Clancy was born in September 1869 in New York State[11], and died September 22, 1941 in Indianapolis, Indiana[12].

vi. Margaret Clancy was born about 1868[13] in New York State. Margaret was alive in 1880 and not alive in 1911 when her mother died.

---

[6] Obituary Utica Newspaper October 23, 1925
[7] Obituary Utica Newspaper October 23, 1925
[8] 1870 and 1880 Redfield, Oswego County, Census
[9] Obituary Utica Newspaper July 12, 1923
[10] Obituary Utica Newspaper July 12, 1923
[11] 1900 Utica New York Census, Ward 9
[12] Obituary Utica Newspaper September 23, 1941
[13] 1870 Redfield, Oswego County, Census

vii.   Ella Clancy was born December 25, 1869 in Redfield, New York[14] and died January 03, 1955 in Faxton Hospital, Utica, New York[15].   She married William Nelson, August 18, 1913 in Utica, New York. Ella lived at 1406 Sunset Avenue in Utica at the time of her death and never had children. She was sometimes called Nell. She was

listed as a weaver in the 1900 Utica, New York Census. She had been educated in Redfield, New York and came to Utica at an early age. She was a communicant of St. Patrick's Church. She and her husband are buried in the Green Lawn Cemetery, New Hartford, New York.[16]

Photo of Ella Clancy from the collection of Pat Farrell and used with permission.

viii.   John H. Clancy was born in August 1873 in Redfield, New York,[17] and died February 20, 1916 at 504 Sunset Ave., Utica, New York[18]. John was a mill hand in the 1900 Utica, New York Census and a bartender in 1915 Utica, New York Census. John died suddenly at the home of his sister, Mrs. William Nelson. He was a bartender at the time of his death and a member of St. Patrick's Church, Utica, New York. He was not married.

5.   ix.   William Edward Clancy was born April 12, 1874 in Oswego County, New York[19] and died February 10, 1948 in Oriskany, New York[20].

6.   x.   James H. Clancy was born October 22, 1874 in Redfield, New York[21] and died October 24, 1910 in Faxton Hospital, Utica, New York[22].

7.   xi.   Anna Clancy was born September 17, 1881 in Redfield, New York[23] and died February 10, 1953 in St. Elizabeth Hospital, Utica, New York[24].

[14] Obituary Utica Newspaper January 4, 1955
[15] Obituary Utica Newspaper January 4, 1955
[16] Green Lawn Cemetery, New Hartford, New York
[17] 1900 Utica New York Census, Ward 9
[18] Obituary Utica Newspaper February 21, 1916
[19] World War I draft registration on Ancestry.com
[20] Obituary Utica Newspaper February 11, 1948
[21] Obituary Utica Newspaper October 25, 1910
[22] Obituary Utica Newspaper October 25, 1910
[23] Obituary Utica Newspaper February 11, 1953
[24] Obituary Utica Newspaper February 11, 1953

Generation Two

2. Hannah Clancy[2] (John H. Clancy[1]) was born on February 15, 1857 in Redfield, New York[25] and died on October 22, 1925 in Utica, New York[26]. She married Hiram Allen in 1880. He was born in December 1847 in Lorraine, New York[27] and died on August 20, 1893 in Utica, New York[28]. She later married Frederick O. Allen on February 07, 1903 in Utica, New York. He was born on December 02, 1859 in Redfield, New York[29] and died on October 11, 1925 in Utica, New York[30]. In the 1860 Redfield, New York Census,

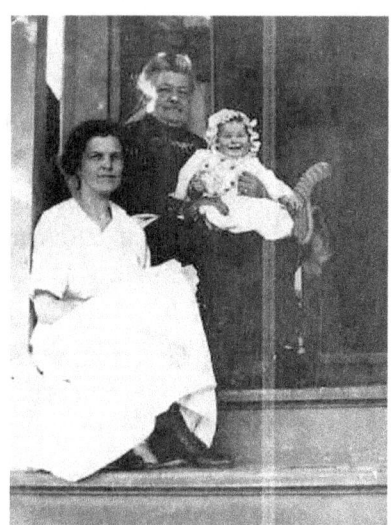

Hannah's name was Honora and she was listed as being 3 years old. That would make her date of birth in 1857 not 1859 as her obituary said. In the 1870 Redfield, New York Census, she was listed as 13 years old. In the 1880 Redfield, New York census, she was listed as 23. Therefore, I believe she was born in 1857 not 1859. Hannah had been in ill health for about six years. She came to Utica in 1885 with her family. She was a member of St. Patrick's Church. The 1900 Ward 3 City of Utica Census indicated Hannah had 6 children, with 5 of them still living. She lived at 904 Green Street, Utica, New York, according to the 1925 Utica Census (9th Ward). Fred was employed for some time at the courthouse. He attended St. George's Church. He was listed as a teamster in 1915.

Photo of Hannah Clancy, her daughter Mary Allen Miller and granddaughter Marjorie Bernadette Miller from the collection of Kevin Miller and used with permission.

Hannah Clancy and Hiram Allen had the following children:

     i.   William Henry Allen was born October 18, 1881 in Redfield, New York[31] and died March 07, 1965 in Utica, New York[32]. He married Clara McCormick on June 26, 1903 in Utica, New York. William was a retired wheelwright for the O. W. Mott Co. and lived at 1626 St. Agnes Avenue at the time of his death.

---

[25] Obituary Utica Newspaper October 23, 1925
[26] Obituary Utica Newspaper October 23, 1925
[27] Family information from Kevin Miller
[28] Family information from Kevin Miller
[29] Family information from Kevin Miller
[30] Family information from Kevin Miller
[31] Family information from Kevin Miller
[32] Family information from Kevin Miller

8.   ii.   Mary Elizabeth Allen was born September 23, 1883 in Redfield, New York[33] and died January 10, 1975 in Utica, New York[34].

9.   iii.   George Frederick Allen was born April 01, 1891 in Utica, New York[35] and died March 26, 1969 in St. Luke's Hospital, New Hartford, New York[36].

Hannah Clancy and Frederick O. Allen had the following children:

10.   i.   Mabel Marguerite Allen was born February 20, 1895 in Utica, New York[37] and died December 17, 1951 in St. Luke's Hospital, Utica, New York[38].

11.   ii.   Helen Magdalen Allen was born September 11, 1898 in Utica, New York[39] and died May 24, 1957 in New York City, New York[40].

12.   iii.   Edwin Joseph Allen was born July 12, 1902 in Utica, New York[41] and died November 29, 1971 in Richmond, California[42].

Photo of Mabel Marguerite Allen from the collection of Donna DeBonzo and used with permission.

3. Mary Etta Clancy[2] (John H. Clancy[1]) was born on August 09, 1864 in Redfield, New York[43] and died on July 11, 1923[44] at 1210 Churchill Avenue, Utica, New York. She married George L. Foote Jr. on December 27, 1888 in Utica, New York, the son of George L. Foote Sr. and Lydia M. Leigh. He was born on January 15, 1863 in Madison, New York[45] and died on June 14, 1945 in Utica, New York[46]. For more on George L. Foote, Jr. see Chapter Two.

Photo of Mary Etta Clancy, age 20, from the author's collection.

---

[33] Family information from Kevin Miller
[34] Obituary Utica Newspaper January 11, 1975
[35] New York State Vital Records
[36] Obituary Utica Newspaper March 27, 1969
[37] Obituary Utica Newspaper December 17, 1951
[38] Obituary Utica Newspaper December 17, 1951
[39] Family information from Kevin Miller
[40] Obituary Utica Newspaper May 25, 1957
[41] California Death Index
[42] California Death Index
[43] Obituary Utica Newspaper July 12, 1923
[44] Obituary Utica Newspaper July 12, 1923
[45] Obituary Utica Newspaper June 15, 1945
[46] Obituary Utica Newspaper June 15, 1945

Mary lived with her daughter, Edna Hickey, at time of her death at 1210 Churchill Avenue, Utica, New York. She was a member of St. Patrick's Church, Utica, New York and lived in Utica for 37 years.

Mary Etta Clancy and George L. Foote Jr had the following children:

13.   i.   Mary Agnes Foote was born August 16, 1890 in Utica, New York and died March 27, 1982 in Lakeland, Florida.[47]

14.   ii.   Isabel L. Foote was born January 08, 1894 in Milford, Massachusetts and died August 31, 1973 in New Hartford, New York[48].

          iii.   Edna Foote was born January 11, 1897 in Utica, New York and died September 22, 1987 in Lakeland, Florida[49]. She married Edward James Hickey in June 1916 in St. Patrick's Church, Utica, New York[50]. For more on Edna Foote, see Chapter Two.

4. Jane (Jennie) E. Clancy[2] (John H. Clancy[1]) was born in September 1869 in New York State[51] and died on September 22, 1941 in Indianapolis, Indiana[52]. She married Michael Burlbach on January 30, 1889 in St. Joseph's Church, Utica, New York[53], the son of Bernard and Catherine Burlbach. He was born in April 1870 in New York State[54] and died in April 1926[55]. Jennie lived with her grandparents (The Donovan's) in Osceola in the 1880 Lewis County Census. Jennie and Michael lived in Vienna in the 1910 Census. In 1912 Jennie and Michael owned and operated the Windsor Hotel in Sylvan Beach, New York. They lived in Albany in 1914 and 1916. In the 1920 Harrisburg Census, Jennie was listed as J. E. Clancy and her daughter, Irene lived with her. Jennie was a waitress and Irene was a keeper in a restaurant. Jennie lived in Harrisburg, Pennsylvania in 1925. In the 1900 Utica Census, Michael was listed as a clothing cutter.

Jane (Jennie) E. Clancy and Michael Burlbach had the following children:

          i.   Gertrude Catherine Burlbach was born in October 1890 in New York State[56] and died June 21, 1910 in Sylvan Beach, New York[57]. She married Wilfred A. Griffin on November 15, 1909 in St. John's Church, Utica, New York[58]. In the wedding announcement of Gertrude and Wilfred, it stated that they were going to make their home

---

[47] Obituary Utica Newspaper March 28, 1982
[48] Obituary Utica Newspaper September 1, 1973
[49] Obituary Utica Newspaper September 23, 1987
[50] Wedding Announcement, Utica Newspaper
[51] 1900 Utica Census, Ward 9
[52] Obituary Utica Newspaper September 23, 1941
[53] Wedding Announcement, Utica Newspaper
[54] 1900 Utica Census, Ward 9
[55] Funeral Announcement, Utica Newspaper
[56] 1900 Utica Census, Ward 9
[57] Death Announcement, Utica Newspaper June 22, 1910
[58] Wedding Announcement, Utica Newspaper

in Montana and were leaving on the train right after the wedding. Gertrude died when her row boat capsized in Oneida Lake. She had only been married a few months.

    ii.   Ethel Burlbach was born in March 1894 in New York State[59].

    iii.   Irene Burlbach was born December 14, 1899 in Utica, New York[60].

5. William Edward Clancy[2] (John H. Clancy[1]) was born on April 12, 1874 in Oswego County, New York[61] and died on February 10, 1948 in Oriskany, New York[62]. He married Helen I. (Nellie) Patterson on April 10, 1914 in St. Peter's Church, Rome, New York. She was born in 1891[63] and died on January 16, 1943 in Rome, New York[64]. William lived in Oriskany in 1923. In the 1925 Census, William was listed as a buffer. He played first base baseball for the Pittsburg Pirates from 1901 to 1905 in the National League making $2800 per year. At the age of 26 he managed Montreal in the International League and during his baseball career wore the uniforms of Rochester and Buffalo in the International League and Oakland, California in the Pacific Coast League.

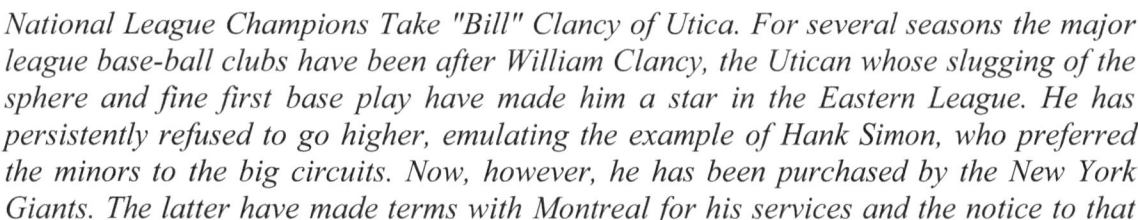

William began his baseball career in 1898 when he joined the pitching staff of the Utica Actives. He later played with Potsdam where he shifted to first base, and then entered the International League where his batting average was over 300. In more recent years, he was a deputy sheriff. He also was employed by the Rome Manufacturing Company Division of Revere Copper and Brass for many years. He was a member of St. Stephen's Church, Oriskany, New York.

Photo of William Clancy when he played baseball for the Pittsburg Pirates in the author's collection.

Saturday Evening Globe - September 6, 1904 SOLD TO THE GIANTS

National League Champions Take "Bill" Clancy of Utica. For several seasons the major league base-ball clubs have been after William Clancy, the Utican whose slugging of the sphere and fine first base play have made him a star in the Eastern League. He has persistently refused to go higher, emulating the example of Hank Simon, who preferred the minors to the big circuits. Now, however, he has been purchased by the New York Giants. The latter have made terms with Montreal for his services and the notice to that

---

[59] 1900 Utica Census, Ward 9
[60] Birth Announcement, Utica Newspaper December 15, 1899
[61] World War I draft registration on Ancestry.com
[62] New York State Vital Records
[63] 1920 Utica Census
[64] Death Announcement, Utica Newspaper January 17, 1943

effect has been promulgated by Farrell. Inasmuch as McGann is under an indefinite suspension it may be that the champions of the National League want the Utican for first base at once.

William Edward Clancy and Helen I. (Nellie) Patterson had the following children:

15.   i.   Mary Velma Clancy was born September 06, 1915 in Forestport, New York[65] and died July 18, 2005 in Mesa, Arizona[66].

ii.   William L. Clancy was born February 14, 1920 in Oriskany, New York[67] and died June 03, 1969 in Faxton Hospital, Utica, New York[68]. William Clancy never married. He worked for the General Cable Corporation before his illness. Prior to that, he was employed by the Rome Turney Radiator Company. He graduated from Rome Free Academy and was a pitcher for the RFA baseball team.

16.   iii.   James C. Clancy was born May 08, 1921[69].

17.   iv.   John E. Clancy was born December 22, 1922 in Oriskany, New York[70] and died August 21, 1987[71] in Faxton Hospital, Utica, New York.

18.   v.   Corinne K. Clancy was born March 4, 1925 in Camden, New York and died February 25, 2010[72].

6. James H. Clancy[2] (John H. Clancy[1]) was born on October 22, 1874 in Redfield, New York[73] and died on October 24, 1910 in Faxton Hospital, Utica, New York[74]. He married Anna A. McClelland on August 27, 1897 in Whitesboro, New York and was divorced in 1904[75]. She was born in February 1879[76].   James came to Utica as a boy. He learned bridge construction work and was employed on the New York Central and Hudson River Railroads. He was a well know athlete. He was an electrician by trade. On October 23, 1910 he was severely scalded when one of the caps on a high pressure steam pipe in the plant of Utica Gas & Electric Company at the foot of Washington Street blew off. He was a member of St. Patrick's Church, Utica, New York and as a young man he took a prominent part in local athletic events and displayed ability of a high order. His divorce announcement was in the Utica Paper and was dated May 7, 1904.

---

[65] Family information from Velma Kidder
[66] Social Security Death Index at Ancestry.com
[67] Obituary Utica Newspaper June 4, 1969
[68] Obituary Utica Newspaper June 4, 1969
[69] Family information from Velma Kidder
[70] Obituary Utica Newspaper August 22, 1987
[71] Obituary Utica Newspaper August 22, 1987
[72] Obituary Utica Newspaper February 26, 2010
[73] Obituary Utica Newspaper October 25, 1910
[74] Obituary Utica Newspaper October 25, 1910
[75] Divorce announcement, Utica Newspaper
[76] 1900 Whitestown, New York Census

James H. Clancy and Anna A. McClelland had the following child:

     i.   Harold James Clancy was born January 01, 1900 in Utica, New York[77] and died in May 1965[78]. Harold lived with his mother at 508 Catherine Street, Utica, New York in 1918 when he registered for the draft.

7. Anna Clancy[2] (John H. Clancy[1]) was born on September 17, 1881 in Redfield, New York[79] and died on February 10, 1953 in St. Elizabeth Hospital, Utica, New York[80]. She married James W. Roberts on June 21, 1904 in St. Patrick's Church, Utica, New York, the son of John Eli Roberts and Catherine Thomas. He was born in 1880 in Utica, New York[81] and died on July 04, 1938 in St. Elizabeth Hospital, Utica, New York[82]. Anna lived at 1001 Walnut Street, Utica, New York at the time of her death. She was listed as a knitting mill hand in the 1900 Utica Census. She was a communicant of St. Patrick's Church.

James had attended Utica schools. He worked eight years for the Utica Gas and Electric Company, 24 years for the Schiller Motors, and for the last two years with the transportation department of the Central New York Power Corporation. The 1910 Census indicated he lived on Wiley Street and was a machinist. The 1920 Census showed him living at 1523 Lincoln Avenue, Utica and working as a superintendent in a garage. The family lived in Albany in the 1930 census.

Photo of Anna Clancy and James Roberts from the collection of Pat Farrell and used with permission.

Anna Clancy and James W. Roberts had the following children:

     i.   James W. Roberts Jr. was born in 1906 in New York State[83]. In 1953 James was living in Syracuse, New York.

---

[77] World War I draft registration on Ancestry.com
[78] Social Security Death Index at Ancestry.com
[79] Obituary Utica Newspaper February 11, 1953
[80] Obituary Utica Newspaper February 11, 1953
[81] Obituary Utica Newspaper July 5, 1938
[82] Obituary Utica Newspaper July 5, 1938
[83] 1920 Utica Census,, Ward 11

19.   ii.   Florence Roberts was born February 11, 1906 in New York State[84] and died February 3, 2000[85] in San Diego, California.

iii.   Howard Roberts was born August 16, 1908 in Utica, New York[86] and died November 01, 1931 in Amsterdam, New York[87].   Howard died in an automobile crash along with his friend, George Wood, in Amsterdam, New York. He attended Utica Free Academy and lived in Albany, New York for the past two years. He was employed by the Philco Battery Service. He was a member of Our Lady of Lourdes Church, Utica, New York.

20.   iv.   John (Jack) Gifford Roberts was born in 1913 in Utica, New York[88] and died June 03, 1990 in St. Elizabeth Hospital, Utica, New York[89].

Photo of Ella (Nell) Clancy, Anna Clancy Roberts with her children Howard, James and Florence taken about 1909 from the collection of Pat Farrell and used with permission.

Photo of John Gifford Roberts in the collection of Diane Techmanski and used with permission.

v.   Walter S. Roberts was born 1915 in Utica, New York[90] and died October 03, 1962 in St. Elizabeth Hospital, Utica, New York[91]. He married Margaret Woodburn in March 1953[92]. Walter was educated in Utica schools. He was a veteran of World War II and served in the Army from 1942 to 1945. He saw service in Algeria and French Morocco. He was employed for many years by Dick Smith's Restaurant in West Utica. Prior to that, he was employed by the Firestone Tire Company and C. J. Fletcher, Inc. He did not have any children.

---

[84] Social Security Death Index at Ancestry.com
[85] Social Security Death Index at Ancestry.com
[86] Obituary Utica Newspaper, November 2, 1931
[87] Obituary Utica Newspaper, November 2, 1931
[88] Obituary Utica Newspaper, June 4, 1990
[89] Obituary Utica Newspaper, June 4, 1990
[90] 1920 Utica Census,, Ward 11
[91] Obituary Utica Newspaper, October 4, 1962
[92] Obituary Utica Newspaper, October 4, 1962

Photo of Walter S. Roberts and his wife Margaret Woodburn from the collection of Diane Techmanski and used with permission.

21.   vi.   E. Gardner Roberts was born in 1926 in Utica, New York[93] and died July 21, 1991 in University Hospital, Syracuse, New York[94].

       vii.   Girl Roberts was born October 04, 1910.

Photo taken in 1920 of Ann Clancy Roberts, James Roberts and children: Howard and James Roberts. This photo was in the collection of Pat Farrell and used with permission.

Photo of Ann Clancy Roberts and son, James Roberts from the collection of Gardy Roberts and used with permission.

---

[93] Obituary Utica Newspaper, July 22, 1991
[94] Obituary Utica Newspaper, July 22, 1991

Generation Three

8. Mary Elizabeth Allen[3] (Hannah Clancy[2], John H. Clancy[1]) was born on September 23, 1883 in Redfield, New York[95] and died on January 10, 1975 in Utica, New York[96]. She married Frederick Mathias Miller on April 24, 1911 in St. Patrick's Church, Utica, New  York, the son of Charles Miller and Mary Schreiber. He was born on December 02, 1882 in Utica, New York[97] and died on March 27, 1950 at 824 Watson Place, Utica, New York[98].   Mary attended school in Utica, New York. She was a member of Our Lady of Lourdes Church, Utica, New York. Frederick was a brakeman for the O & W Railroad, retiring in 1947. He was a member of the Brotherhood of Railroad Trainmen and attended St. Patrick's Church.

Photo of Mary Elizabeth Allen Miller taken in 1969 at her granddaughter's wedding. From the collection of Gail Baldwin and used with permission.

Mary Elizabeth Allen and Frederick Mathias Miller had the following children:

　　　　i.　　　　Clifford Allen Miller was born February 19, 1912 in Utica, New York[99] and died February 03, 1943 in the North Atlantic[100]. Clifford was killed in action in the North Atlantic on the ship, Dorchester, during WW II. Clifford graduated from Utica Free Academy in 1930 and worked for the A & P Grocery Store in Utica. He was inducted into the Navy in July of 1942 and graduated from the Radio Technical School at Scott Field, Illinois.

22.　　ii.　　　　Marjorie Bernadette Miller was born August 20, 1914 in Utica, New York[101] and died December 08, 2000 in St. Elizabeth Medical Center, Utica, New York[102].

　　　　iii.　　　Jeanette Elizabeth Miller was June 27, 1916 in Utica, New York[103] and died May 08, 1931 in Utica, New York[104].

23.　　iv.　　　Robert Vincent Miller was born December 23, 1918 in Utica, New York and died June 01, 1984 in Faxton Hospital, Utica, New York[105].

---

[95] Family information form Kevin Miller
[96] Obituary Utica Newspaper, January 11, 1975
[97] Obituary Utica Newspaper, March 28, 1950
[98] Obituary Utica Newspaper, March 28, 1950
[99] Family information form Kevin Miller
[100] Family information form Kevin Miller
[101] Obituary Utica Newspaper, December 9, 2000
[102] Obituary Utica Newspaper, December 9, 2000
[103] Family information form Kevin Miller
[104] Family information form Kevin Miller
[105] Obituary Utica Newspaper, June 2, 1984

v.   Gertrude Marie Miller was born July 21, 1921 in Utica, New York[106]

9. George Frederick Allen[3] (Hannah Clancy[2], John H. Clancy[1]) was born on April 01, 1891 in Utica, New York[107] and died on March 26, 1969 in St. Luke's Hospital, New Hartford, New York[108]. He married Anna Belle Millington on September 10, 1917 in Utica, New York, the daughter of John Millington and Anna Snyder. She was born on March 01, 1893 in Utica, New York[109] and died on January 23, 1974 in St. Elizabeth Hospital, Utica, New York[110]. George was a retired electrician who worked for Langdon-Hughes Construction Company, retiring in 1967. He was a World War II veteran and a member of St. Paul's Church. Belle attended Utica Schools and had lived in Whitesboro for 33 years. She was a member of St. Paul's Church, its Women's Club and Whitestown American Legion Auxiliary.

George Frederick Allen and Anna Belle Millington had the following children:
i.   Doris Marie (Sister Marilyn) Allen was born November 21, 1918 in Utica, New York[111]. She was a Sister OSF Third Order of St. Francis, Syracuse, New York.
24. ii.   Virginia Helen Allen was born May 20, 1920 in Utica, New York[112] and died December 25, 1998 in Whitesboro, New York[113].
25. iii.   Edna A. Allen was born November 14, 1921 in Utica, New York[114] and died June 25, 2010 in the Presbyterian Nursing Home, New Hartford, New York[115].
26. iv.   George Frederick Allen Jr was born May 04, 1923 in Utica, New York[116] and died December 02, 2002 in Rome Memorial Hospital, Rome, New York[117].
27. v.   John Millington Allen was born February 28, 1929 in Utica, New York and died February 11, 2008 in St. Elizabeth Medical Center, Utica, New York

---

[106] Family information form Kevin Miller
[107] New York State Vital Records
[108] Obituary Utica Newspaper, March 27, 1969
[109] Obituary Utica Newspaper, January 24, 1974
[110] Obituary Utica Newspaper, January 24, 1974
[111] Family information form Kevin Miller
[112] Obituary Utica Newspaper, December 26, 1998
[113] Obituary Utica Newspaper, December 26, 1998
[114] Obituary Utica Newspaper, June 28, 2010
[115] Obituary Utica Newspaper, June 28, 2010
[116] Obituary Utica Newspaper, December 3, 2002
[117] Obituary Utica Newspaper, December 3, 2002

10. Mabel Marguerite Allen[3] (Hannah Clancy[2], John H. Clancy[1]) was born on February 20, 1895 in Utica, New York[118] and died on December 17, 1951 in St. Luke's Hospital, Utica, New York[119]. She married George Maine Steffen on June 18, 1919 in Utica, New York, the son of August Steffen and Helene Maine. He was born on April 09, 1894 in Utica, New York[120] and died on May 29, 1971 in Boonville, New York[121]. Mable was listed as an office assistant in the 1915 Utica Census. She was a communicant of Our Lady of Lourdes Church and a member of the Ladies of Charity of St. John's Home and of the DFO Club.

Photo of Mabel Marguerite Allen taken February 20, 1913 for her high school graduation from the collection of Donna DeBonzo and used with permission.

George was a graduate of Utica Free Academy, Utica, New York and was a World War I Army veteran, having served in France. He was employed as a payroll clerk at Beaunit Fibers in Utica, for 23 years. He was later superintendent of buildings at Oneida County Courthouse for 9 years. He retired in 1960. He was a member of the Lutheran Church; the Utica Elks Lodge; and a member of the Charles J. Love Post, American Legion, Boonville, New York.

Mabel Marguerite Allen and George Maine Steffen had the following children:
28.   i.   George Maine Steffen Jr was born October 19, 1921 in Utica, New York[122] and died July 16, 1991 in Whitesboro, New York[123].
29.   ii.   Jean Marie Steffen was born August 07, 1924 in Utica, New York[124] and died November 10, 1985 in Vienna, New York[125].
        iii.   Living Steffen
30.   iv.   Richard James Steffen was born July 27, 1927 in Utica, New York, and died August 15, 2006 in Canastota, New York[126]
31.   v.   Allen Frederick Steffen Sr was born July 27, 1927 in Utica, New York[127] and died April 26, 1973 in California[128].

---

[118] Obituary Utica Newspaper, December 18, 1951
[119] Obituary Utica Newspaper, December 18, 1951
[120] Obituary Utica Newspaper, May 30, 1971
[121] Obituary Utica Newspaper, May 30, 1971
[122] Obituary Utica Newspaper, July 19, 1991
[123] Obituary Utica Newspaper, July 19, 1991
[124] Obituary Utica Newspaper, November 11, 1985
[125] Obituary Utica Newspaper, November 11, 1985
[126] Social Security Death Index at Ancestry.com
[127] California Death Index at Ancestry.com
[128] California Death Index at Ancestry.com

11. Helen Magdalen Allen[3] (Hannah Clancy[2], John H. Clancy[1]) was born on September 11, 1898 in Utica, New York[129] and died on May 24, 1957 in New York City, New York[130]. She married William Patrick Manley on May 12, 1920 in Utica, New York, the son of William Manley and Anna Gallagher. He was born on December 01, 1898 in Utica, New York[131] and died on October 06, 1969 in Faxton Hospital, Utica, New York[132]. William lived in New Hartford and South Daytona Beach, Florida. He had attended Utica schools. He was employed by the International Heating Company for many years retiring in 1963. He was a member of St. Joseph's - St. Patrick's Church. Utica, New York.

Photo of Helen Magdalen Allen with her husband William Patrick Manley taken in 1946 from the collection of Susan Hickox and used with permission.

Helen Magdalen Allen and William Patrick Manley had the following child:

32. i. Donald James Manley was born June 20, 1925 in Utica, New York[133] and died November 24, 1993 in St. Elizabeth Hospital, Utica, New York[134].

Photo of Helen Magdalen Allen with her husband William Patrick Manley, Donald James Manley and his wife Margaret Lubey from the collection of Susan Hickox and used with permission.

12. Edwin Joseph Allen[3] (Hannah Clancy[2], John H. Clancy[1]) was born on July 12, 1902 in Utica, New York[135] and died on November 29, 1971 in Richmond, California[136]. He married Mary Gertrude Rosencranz on February 18, 1924 in Utica, New York, the daughter of August Rosencranz and Alice Down. She was born on December 25, 1902 in Utica, New York[137] and died April 1, 1981 in Utica, New York[138]. Edwin worked in Utica as a chauffeur, but because of marital problems he and Mary were having, he moved to California around 1933. Without divorcing his first wife, he married Bernice in

---

[129] Family information form Kevin Miller
[130] Obituary Utica Newspaper, May 25, 1957
[131] Obituary Utica Newspaper, October 7, 1969
[132] Obituary Utica Newspaper, October 7, 1969
[133] Obituary Utica Newspaper, November 25, 1933
[134] Obituary Utica Newspaper, November 25, 1933
[135] California Death Index at Ancestry.com
[136] California Death Index at Ancestry.com
[137] Obituary Utica Newspaper, April 2, 1981
[138] Obituary Utica Newspaper, April 2, 1981

California and they had at least five children.

Edwin Joseph Allen and Mary Gertrude Rosencranz had the following children:

33.   i.   Edward Arnold Allen was born October 28, 1924 in Utica, New York[139] and died January 19, 1988 in New Hartford, New York[140].

34.   ii.   John Frederick Allen was born May 26, 1926 in Utica, New York[141] and died January 19, 2006 in St. Lukes Memorial Hospital, New Hartford, New York[142].

    iii.   Living Allen

13. Mary Agnes Foote[3] (Mary Etta Clancy[2], John H. Clancy[1]) was born on August 16, 1890 in Utica, New York and died on March 27, 1982 in Lakeland, Florida.[143]   She married Alcide F. Emery on July 14, 1909 in St. Patrick's Church, Utica, New York[144] the son of Jean (John) Baptist Emery and Celina Gagnier. He was born on May 18, 1885 in

Stoney Point, Ontario, Canada[145] and died on July 12, 1961 in Utica, New York[146]. For more on Mary Agnes Foote, see Chapter Two. For more on Alcide F. Emery, see Chapter One.

Mary Agnes Foote and Alcide F. Emery had the following children:

35.   i.   Harold Alcide Emery was born July 21, 1913 in Utica, New York and died December 11, 1989 in New Hartford, New York[147].

36.   **ii.**   **Gordon Charles Emery** was born March 29, 1915 in Utica, New York[148] and died October 09, 1981 in Utica, New York. [149]

Photo of Mary Agnes Foote, age 20 and Alcide F. Emery, age 25 from the authors collection.

[139] Family information form Kevin Miller
[140] Family information form Kevin Miller
[141] Obituary Utica Newspaper, January 20, 2006
[142] Obituary Utica Newspaper, January 20, 2006
[143] Death Certificate
[144] Wedding Announcement, Utica Newspaper
[145] Obituary Utica Newspaper, July 13, 1961
[146] Obituary Utica Newspaper, July 13, 1961
[147] Obituary Utica Newspaper, December 12, 1989
[148] Death Certificate
[149] Death Certificate

14. Isabel Lydia Foote[3] (Mary Etta Clancy[2], John H. Clancy[1]) was born on January 08, 1894[150] in Milford, Massachusetts and died on August 31, 1973 in New Hartford, New York.[151] For more on Isabel Lydia Foote, see Chapter Two.

15. Mary Velma Clancy[3] (William Edward Clancy[2], John H. Clancy[1]) was born on September 06, 1915 in Forestport, New York[152] and died on July 18, 2005 in Mesa, Arizona[153]. She married Justin Lyman in 1937, Frank Aquino in 1945 and Harry Kidder in 1955. Mary Velma Clancy was born two months early and weighed 2 1/4 lbs. She fit in a cigar box. Her mother had gone with her father to Forestport, New York to hunt in September 1915. Velma's mother went into labor. Her father went to a nearby house to get a doctor to come to his wife's aide. The doctor's wife told him the doctor was on vacation and not working. William aimed his gun at the woman and demanded the doctor come with him immediately. The doctor did go and delivered the baby. Velma slept in a drawer for a few months. They stayed in Forestport for the winter and returned home in the early spring. Mary Velma Clancy and Justin Lyman had three children who may still be living. Mary Velma Clancy and Frank Aquino had one child who may still be living. Mary Velma Clancy and Harry Kidder had one child who may still be living.

16. James C. Clancy[3] (William Edward Clancy[2], John H. Clancy[1]) was born on May 08, 1921[154]. He married Elizabeth Rocker. They had one child who may still be living.

17. John E. Clancy[3] (William Edward Clancy[2], John H. Clancy[1]) was born on December 22, 1922 in Oriskany, New York[155] and died on August 21, 1987 in Faxton Hospital, Utica, New York.[156] He married Alice Ramsdale on July 21, 1951 in Taberg, New York. John attended school in Oriskany and Rome, New York. He served in the Army in World War II and became a disabled veteran. John E. Clancy and Alice Ramsdale had three children who may still be living.

---

[150] Obituary Utica Newspaper, September 1, 1973
[151] Obituary Utica Newspaper, September 1, 1973
[152] Social Security Death Index at Ancestry.com
[153] Social Security Death Index at Ancestry.com
[154] 1925 Whitestown, New York Census
[155] Obituary Utica Newspaper, August 22, 1987
[156] Obituary Utica Newspaper, August 22, 1987

18. Kathryn Corrine Clancy[3] (William Edward Clancy[2], John H. Clancy[1]) was born March 4, 1925 and died February 25, 2010[157]. She married Neil W. Engle in April 21, 1947 in Oriskany Falls, New York[158]. He was born on March 09, 1909 in Oriskany, New York[159] and died on September 26, 1980 in Community Memorial Hospital, Hamilton, New York[160]. Corinne received her education at Rome Free Academy, Rome, New York. She retired from the Madison Post Office in 1975. She was the past president of the Oriskany Falls Firemen's Auxiliary, a member of St. Joseph's Catholic Church and enjoyed years of volunteer service at Community Memorial Hospital. Neil had been employed by the Rome Development Center retiring in 1973. He was a 39-year member and past fire chief of the Oriskany Falls Volunteer Fire Department.   They had three children who may still be living.

19. Florence Roberts[3] (Anna Clancy[2], John H. Clancy[1]) was born February 11, 1906 in New York State[161] and died February 3, 2000 in San Diego, California[162]. She married Edward James Horan. He was born October 24, 1906 and died January 22, 1979 in San Diego, California. They lived in Syracuse in 1953.

Photo of Florence Roberts Horan and her husband Edward from the collection of Diane Techmanski and used with permission.

20. John (Jack) Gifford Roberts[3] (Anna Clancy[2], John H. Clancy[1]) was born in 1913 in Utica, New York[163] and died on June 03, 1990 in St. Elizabeth Hospital, Utica, New York[164]. He married Mary Agnes Hahn on October 04, 1939 in St. Joseph's Church, Utica, New York. She was born in 1918 in Utica, New York[165] and died on June 29, 1988 in 922 Stark Street, Utica, New York[166]. For many years, John was a self-employed photographer and was the owner of the Hahn and Roberts Commercial Photography. He was also later employed at Tracy-Adams Photo. He was a member of St. Joseph's St. Patrick's Church, Utica, New York. Mary had been employed by Tracy-Adams, Inc. of Utica and was a member of St. Joseph's St. Patrick's Church. John (Jack) G. Roberts and Mary Agnes Hahn had five children who may still be living.

[157] Obituary Utica Newspaper, February 26, 2010
[158] Obituary Utica Newspaper, February 26, 2010
[159] Obituary Utica Newspaper, September 27, 1980
[160] Obituary Utica Newspaper, September 27, 1980
[161] Social Security Death Index at Ancestry.com
[162] Social Security Death Index at Ancestry.com
[163] Obituary Utica Newspaper, June 4, 1990
[164] Obituary Utica Newspaper, June 4, 1990
[165] Obituary Utica Newspaper, June 30, 1988
[166] Obituary Utica Newspaper, June 30, 1988

Photo of Ann Clancy Roberts with her sons, John, Walter and Gardner Roberts from the collection of Pat Farrell and used with permission.

21. E. Gardner Roberts[3] (Anna Clancy[2], John H. Clancy[1]) was born in 1926 in Utica, New York[167] and died on July 21, 1991 in University Hospital, Syracuse, New York[168]. He married Gertrude V. Morse on October 21, 1947 in St. Patrick's Church, Utica, New York[169]. "Gardy" had lived in Syracuse for the past 25 years. He was retired from Ford Motor Credit in Dewitt after 23 years of service. He had previously been the Branch

Manager for Commercial Credit in Utica for 16 years. He had received his B.A. in Business Administration from Utica College of Syracuse University and had served in combat while in the Navy during World War II.   E. Gardner Roberts and Gertrude V. Morse had two children who may still be living.

Photo of Edward Gardner Roberts from the collection of Diane Techmanski and used with permission.

---

[167] Obituary Utica Newspaper, July 22, 1991
[168] Obituary Utica Newspaper, July 22, 1991
[169] Obituary Utica Newspaper, July 22, 1991

Generation Four

22. Marjorie Bernadette Miller[4] (Mary Elizabeth Allen[3], Hannah Clancy[2], John H. Clancy[1]) was born on August 20, 1914 in Utica, New York[170] and died on December 08, 2000 in St. Elizabeth Medical Center, Utica, New York[171]. She married George Hiram Wilson on October 19, 1946 in St. Patrick's Church, Utica, New York, the son of Freeman Wilson and Flora Silvernail. He was born on March 28, 1918 in Masonville, New York[172] and died on December 31, 1978 in St. Elizabeth Hospital, Utica, New York[173]. Marjorie took great pride in being a home maker. She was a member of St.

 Thomas Church, New Hartford, New York. George was educated in Sidney schools and came to Utica in 1942. For many years he was a partner in the Burns and Wilson Garage in New Hartford and at the time of his death, he was employed by the Murphy Excavating Company. He had five grandchildren at the time of his death. Marjorie Bernadette Miller and George Hiram Wilson had three children who may still be living.

Photo of Marjorie Bernadette Miller Wilson and her mother Mary Elizabeth Allen Miller taken in 1970. From the collection of Gail Baldwin and used with permission.

23. Robert Vincent Miller[4] (Mary Elizabeth Allen[3], Hannah Clancy[2], John H. Clancy[1]) was born on December 23, 1918 in Utica, New York[174] and died on June 01, 1984 in Faxton Hospital, Utica, New York[175]. He was married on June 24, 1950 in Utica, New York.[176]. Robert was educated in Utica schools. For over 30 years he lived in New Hartford. During World War II he served in the United States Navy in the European and Mediterranean Theaters, and was a recipient of the Purple Heart. He had been employed by the A & P Company in Clinton for over 30 years. He was a member of St. Thomas Church, New Hartford, and was an avid bowler in the Utica area. Robert Vincent Miller and his wife had three children who may still be living.

---

[170] Obituary Utica Newspaper, December 9, 2000
[171] Obituary Utica Newspaper, December 9, 2000
[172] Obituary Utica Newspaper, January 1, 1979
[173] Obituary Utica Newspaper, January 1, 1979
[174] Obituary Utica Newspaper, June 2, 1984
[175] Obituary Utica Newspaper, June 2, 1984
[176] Family information form Kevin Miller

24. Virginia Helen Allen[4] (George Frederick Allen[3], Hannah Clancy[2], John H. Clancy[1]) was born on May 20, 1920 in Utica, New York[177] and died on December 25, 1998 in Whitesboro, New York[178]. She married Robert Faulkner Horigan on April 26, 1941 in Utica, New York, the son of James Horigan and Rena Pryor. He was born on August 04, 1918 in Whitesboro, New York[179] and died on March 06, 1986 in Whitesboro, New York[180]. Robert received his education in Whitesboro Schools. He was a World War II Army Veteran serving with the 42nd Rainbow Division overseas. He was a member of St. Paul's Church, American Legion Post #1113, The Town of Webb VFW, and was Scout Master of the Explorer Scouts for many years. He was a printing officer at Griffiss Air Force Base before retiring in 1979.

Virginia Helen Allen and Robert Faulkner Horigan had the following child:

     i.   Allen Michael Horigan was born December 25, 1946[181] and died October 26, 1980[182].

25. Edna A. Allen[4] (George Frederick Allen[3], Hannah Clancy[2], John H. Clancy[1]) was born November 14, 1921 in Utica, New York[183] and died June 25, 2010 at the Presbyterian Nursing Home, New Hartford, New York[184]. She married Bernard V. DeBlois on July 22, 1944 in St. Patrick's Church, Utica, New York[185]. He was born February 13, 1920 and died August 5, 2005 in Whitesboro, New York[186]. Bernard received his education in local schools. He served as a Sergeant in the US Marine Corps with the 1st Battalion, 7th Marines, 1st Marine Division during World War II where he was a runner for General L.B. Puller. Because of his wounds received in action, he was awarded the Purple Heart Medal. He retired from Griffiss Air Force Base. He and Edna were members of St. Paul's Church, Whitesboro, New York.

Edna Allen and Bernard D. DeBlois had the following children:

     i.   Michael Allen DeBlois was born June 23, 1945 at Camp Lejune, North Carolina[187] and died November 18, 2001 in St. Elizabeth Hospital, Utica, New York[188].

     ii.   Living DeBlois

     iii.   Living DeBlois

---

[177] Obituary Utica Newspaper, December 26, 1998
[178] Obituary Utica Newspaper, December 26, 1998
[179] Obituary Utica Newspaper, March 7, 1986
[180] Obituary Utica Newspaper, March 7, 1986
[181] Obituary Utica Newspaper, October 27, 1980
[182] Obituary Utica Newspaper, October 27, 1980
[183] Obituary Utica Newspaper, June 28, 2010
[184] Obituary Utica Newspaper, June 28, 2010
[185] Obituary Utica Newspaper, June 28, 2010
[186] Social Security Death Index at Ancestry.com
[187] Obituary Utica Newspaper, November 19, 2001
[188] Obituary Utica Newspaper, November 19, 2001

26. George Frederick Allen Jr[4] (George Frederick Allen[3], Hannah Clancy[2], John H. Clancy[1]) was born on May 04, 1923 in Utica, New York[189] and died on December 02, 2002 in Rome Memorial Hospital, Rome, New York[190]. He was married on April 26, 1947 in Utica, New York. George lived in Camden, New York since 1968. He retired after 25 years as a printer with Farnsworth Printing in the mid 1980's. He served with the U.S. Army during World War II and was a member of the Arthur S. Moran American Legion Post #66 and the Utica Craftsman Club. He was an avid fisherman and enjoyed camping at Otter Lake. George Frederick Allen Jr. and his wife had three children who may still be living.

27. John Millington Allen[4] (George Frederick Allen[3], Hannah Clancy[2], John H. Clancy[1]) was born February 28, 1929 in Utica, New York and died February 11, 2008 in St. Elizabeth Medical Center, Utica, New York. John was a graduate of Whitesboro Central School and was employed by the State of New York until his retirement. He enjoyed his camp in the Adirondacks where he was fondly known as the Mayor of Otter Lake.

28. George Maine Steffen Jr[4] (Mabel Marguerite Allen[3], Hannah Clancy[2], John H. Clancy[1]) was born on October 19, 1921 in Utica, New York[191] and died on July 16, 1991 in Whitesboro, New York[192].

He married Claire Marie Page on September 09, 1944 in Our Lady of Lourdes Church, Utica, New York[193], the daughter of John Page and Blanche Whittaker. Claire was born October 17, 1925 in Utica, New York and died April 23, 2001 in St. Petersburg, Florida[194]. George lived in Baldwinsville in 1971. He had been employed with the Honeywell Company until his retirement in 1965. He was a member of St. Paul's Church, Whitesboro, New York. He served in the Navy during World War II.

Photo of the wedding of Jean Marie Steffen with her parents Mabel and George Steffen taken September 28, 1946. This photo was in the collection of Donna DeBonzo and used with permission.

George Maine Steffen Jr. and Claire Marie Page had the following children:
  i.   Living Steffen

---

[189] Obituary Utica Newspaper, December 3, 2002
[190] Obituary Utica Newspaper, December 3, 2002
[191] Obituary Utica Newspaper, July 17, 1991
[192] Obituary Utica Newspaper, July 17, 1991
[193] Obituary Utica Newspaper, July 17, 1991
[194] Social Security Death Index at Ancestry.com

ii.   Vickie Elizabeth Steffen was born August 10, 1949 in Albany, New York and died February 12, 1995 in Hillsborough County, Florida. She was married twice. The second time was on July 10, 1975 in Syracuse, New York. She and her first husband had two children who may still be living.

29. Jean Marie Steffen[4] (Mabel Marguerite Allen[3], Hannah Clancy[2], John H. Clancy[1]) was born on August 07, 1924 in Utica, New York[195] and died on November 10, 1985 in Vienna, New York[196]. She married Donald Charles Zimmerman on September 28, 1946 in Utica, New York, the son of Lloyd and Minnie Zimmerman. He was born in 1924 in Oneida, New York[197] and died May 20, 1981 at the Veterans Administration Medical Center, Syracuse, New York[198]. She married Calvin "Dutch" Harrington on June 18, 1971 in Sylvan Beach, New York. Jean was a graduate of Utica Free Academy and attended the Utica School of Commerce. She was of Catholic faith. Jean Marie Steffen and Donald Charles Zimmerman had two children who may still be living.

30. Richard James Steffen[4] (Mabel Marguerite Allen[3], Hannah Clancy[2], John H. Clancy[1]) was born July 27, 1927 in Utica, New York, and died August 15, 2006 in Canastota, New York[199]. He was married on November 7, 1952. He and his wife had two children who may still be living.

31. Allen Frederick Steffen Sr[4] (Mabel Marguerite Allen[3], Hannah Clancy[2], John H. Clancy[1]) was born on July 27, 1927 in Utica, New York[200] and died on April 26, 1973 in California[201]. He was married on November 09, 1957 in Manhattan Beach, California[202].

32. Donald James Manley[4] (Helen Magdalen Allen[3], Hannah Clancy[2], John H. Clancy[1]) was born on June 20, 1925 in Utica, New York[203] and died on November 24, 1993 in St. Elizabeth Hospital, Utica, New York[204]. He married Margaret Lubey on May 25, 1946 in St. Patrick's Church, Utica, New York, the daughter of Edmund Lubey and Margaret Duerheimer. She was born on March 20, 1926 in Utica, New York[205] and died on November 05, 1993 in Crouse Irving Memorial Hospital, Syracuse, New York[206]. Donald lived at 76 Oakdale Avenue, New Hartford, New York, at the time of his death. He had attended Utica schools and graduated from Utica Free Academy.

---

[195] Obituary Utica Newspaper, November 11, 1985
[196] Obituary Utica Newspaper, November 11, 1985
[197] Obituary, Syracuse Newspaper, May 21, 1981
[198] Obituary, Syracuse Newspaper, May 21, 1981
[199] Social Security Death Index at Ancestry.com
[200] California Death Index at Ancestry.com
[201] California Death Index at Ancestry.com
[202] Family information form Kevin Miller
[203] Obituary Utica Newspaper, November 25, 1993
[204] Obituary Utica Newspaper, November 25, 1993
[205] Obituary Utica Newspaper, November 6, 1993
[206] Obituary Utica Newspaper, November 6, 1993

For over 35 years Don was employed at the International Heating and Air Conditioning Company and later the Frederick Group of Utica, retiring in 1980. He was a member of

St. Thomas Church and a member of the Heenan Spiritual Group. Donald was a World War II U.S. Navy Veteran, serving in Europe.

Margaret was raised and educated in Utica and was a graduate of Utica Free Academy, Class of 1943. She was employed at the Utica Mutual Insurance Company, retiring in 1988. She was a member of St. Thomas Church, New Hartford and was an active volunteer at the Presbyterian Home. Donald James Manley and Margaret Lubey had three children who may still be living.

Photo of William James Manley and his wife Margaret Lubey on May 25, 1946 from the collection of Susan Hickox and used with permission.

33. Edward Arnold Allen[4] (Edwin Joseph Allen[3], Hannah Clancy[2], John H. Clancy[1]) was born on October 28, 1924 in Utica, New York[207] and died on January 19, 1988 in New Hartford, New York[208]. He was married on June 14, 1952 in Utica, New York[209].
Arnold served in the U.S. Navy during World War II and the Korean Conflict. He settled in Barneveld after marrying. He was employed by Armor Meat Packing Company and later purchased Allen's Market, the former Houcks Market in Barneveld, retiring in 1986 due to poor health. He was a member of St. David's Episcopal Church, Barneveld, the Remsen Lodge F & A.M. #667, the Cold Brook American Legion, and the Barneveld Fire Company. Edward Arnold Allen and his wife had three children who may still be living.

34. John Frederick Allen[4] (Edwin Joseph Allen[3], Hannah Clancy[2], John H. Clancy[1]) was born on May 26, 1926 in Utica, New York[210] and died on January 19, 2006 in St. Lukes Memorial Hospital, New Hartford, New York[211]. He married Charlotte Hoke Austin in September 1946 in New Hartford, New York, the daughter of Charles L. Hoke and Laura Stanley. She was born on April 01, 1914 in Utica, New York[212]and died on September 13, 1970 in Utica, New York[213]. He later married again on February 27, 1971[214]. John

[207] Obituary Utica Newspaper, January 20, 1988
[208] Obituary Utica Newspaper, January 20, 1988
[209] Obituary Utica Newspaper, January 20, 1988
[210] Obituary Utica Newspaper, January 20, 2006
[211] Obituary Utica Newspaper, January 20, 2006
[212] Obituary Utica Newspaper, September 14, 1970
[213] Obituary Utica Newspaper, September 14, 1970

was a union mason of the Bricklayers Union Local #2 and was formerly employed with Charles A. Gaetano Construction Company.   Charlotte was a graduate of Utica Free Academy and had studied with the late Dr. Frank P. Cavallo, a Utica music instructor. She had at one time been choir director for the Moravian Church of the Good Shepherd, the New Hartford Baptist Church and Dryer Memorial Church. For several years she was a clerk for the Oneida County Department of Public Works, retiring in 1967.   John Frederick Allen and Charlotte Hoke Austin had two children who may still be living.

35. Harold Alcide Emery[4] (Mary Agnes Foote[3], Mary Etta Clancy[2], John H. Clancy[1]) was born on July 21, 1913 in Utica, New York[215] and died on December 11, 1989 in New Hartford, New York.[216] He married Marie Longtin Emery on January 08, 1938 in Utica, New York, the daughter of Paul and Amelia Longtin. She was born on January 29, 1916 in Norristown, Pennsylvania and died on January 01, 1990 in New Hartford, New York. [217]. For more on Harold, see Chapter One.

Photo of Harold and Gordon in 1917 from the author's collection.

36. Gordon Charles Emery[4] (Mary Agnes Foote[3], Mary Etta Clancy[2], John H. Clancy[1]) was born on March 29, 1915 in Utica, New York[218] and died on October 09, 1981 in Utica, New York.[219] He married Gertrude Bowman on April 26, 1941 in St. Joseph's Church, Utica, New York,[220] the daughter of George Francis Bowman and Susanna Etta Sifer. She was born on January 14, 1920 in Utica, New York[221]. For more on Gordon, see Chapter One.

37. Hazel Hart[4] (Isabel L. Foote[3], Mary Etta Clancy[2], John H. Clancy[1]) was born on May 10, 1912 in Morrisville, New York,[222] and died on July 10, 1949 in Memorial Hospital, Utica, New York[223]. She married Ivan Jay Collins on April 29, 1932. He was born in

---

[214] Family information form Kevin Miller
[215] Obituary Utica Newspaper, December 12, 1989
[216] Obituary Utica Newspaper, December 12, 1989
[217] Obituary Utica Newspaper, January 2, 1990
[218] Death Certificate
[219] Death Certificate
[220] Marriage Record, St. Joseph's Church, Utica, New York
[221] Gertrude Emery verbal
[222] Obituary Utica Newspaper, July 11, 1949
[223] Obituary Utica Newspaper, July 11, 1949

1905 in Norwood, New York[224] and died on March 03, 1964 in Elizabeth Hospital, Utica, New York[225]. For more on Hazel, see chapter Two.

38. Howard John Hart (Isabel L. Foote[3], Mary Etta Clancy[2], John H. Clancy[1]) was born on September 16, 1914 in Eaton, New York[226] and died on February 25, 1990 in St. Elizabeth Hospital, Utica, New York[227]. He married Elizabeth Marie Mahlmann on March 31, 1938 in the home of Rev. Walter Leo Bailey, Utica, New York, the daughter of Harry C. Mahlmann and Amelia Kroutch. She was born on December 05, 1918 in Utica, New York[228] and died on October 02, 2008 in Presbyterian Home, New Hartford, New York[229]. For more on Howard, see Chapter Two.

---

[224] Obituary Utica Newspaper, March 4, 1964
[225] Obituary Utica Newspaper, February 26, 1990
[226] Obituary Utica Newspaper, February 26, 1990
[227] Obituary Utica Newspaper, February 26, 1990
[228] Obituary Utica Newspaper, October 3, 2008
[229] Obituary Utica Newspaper, October 3, 2008

Chapter Four

Descendants of Jeremiah Donovan

Generation One

1. Jeremiah Donovan[1] was born in 1800 in County Cork, Ireland[1] and died on August 13, 1888 in Osceola, New York[2]. He married Catherine Coughlin March 3, 1829[3] at St. Finbarrs Church in South Cork, Ireland[4]. She was born in 1811 in Ireland[5]. In the 1850 census, this family was living in Annsville, New York and their name was spelled Dannaven. Jeremiah was listed as a laborer. The 1855 Osceola, New York Census indicated Jeremiah was a naturalized citizen and owner of land. Witnesses to his naturalization were John Moore and Michael Spellecy of Florence, New York. The Naturalization Declaration of Intent signed September 5, 1844 in Oneida County; stated Jeremiah came from County Cork, Ireland. In the 1860 Osceola Census, his name was spelled Donavon and he was listed as a farmer. In the 1870 Osceola Census, his name was spelled Denavan and he was listed as a farmer. In the 1880 Osceola Census, his first name was listed as Timothy and he was listed as a farmer.

Jeremiah died in the Osceola, New York at 9:00 p.m. of inanction. His death certificate came from the Town of Florence and stated he had been in this country for 51 years. That would mean he came to America in 1837. However, his first child was born in 1836 in Amsterdam, New York. He had lived in Osceola for 34 years and was widowed at the time of his death. His occupation was listed as a farmer. His obituary stated he came to this country with his wife and settled in Osceola. He was an honest, industrious man and respected by all who knew him.

In the 1860 Osceola Census, the Donovan's lived next door to Andrew Coughlin. This could be a nephew or younger brother to Catherine Coughlin Donovan.

Jeremiah Donovan and Catherine Coughlin had the following children:
2.   i.   Mary Ann Donovan was born in October 1836 in Amsterdam, New York[6] and died December 12, 1911 in St. Elizabeth Hospital, Utica, New York[7].
    ii.   Daniel Donovan was born in 1839 in Oneida County, New York[8]. Daniel lived in Scranton, Pennsylvania in 1888. When his sister, Catherine, died in 1909, Daniel hadn't been heard from in ten years.

---

[1] Naturalization papers Declaration of Intent dated September 2, 1844, Oneida County, New York
[2] Death Certificate
[3] St. Finbarrs Church Records, South Cork, Ireland at www.churchrecords.irishgenealogy.ie
[4] Obituary Camden Advance Journal, August 23, 1888
[5] 1880 Osceola, New York Census
[6] Obituary, Utica Newspaper December 13, 1911
[7] Obituary, Utica Newspaper December 13, 1911
[8] 1850 Annsville, New York Census

iii.   John Donovan was born in 1841 in Oneida County, New York[9]. John was not alive in 1909 when his sister Catherine died.

3.   iv.   Margaret Donovan was born 1843 in New York State[10] and died March 20, 1925 in Utica, New York[11].

v.   Catherine (Kate) Donovan was born March 15, 1846 in Lewis County, New York[12] and died October 28, 1909 in Osceola or Florence, New York[13]. Her death notice was found in the Camden, New York, newspaper. According to Catherine's will, she had assets of $1798.22 and expenses of $462.69. A niece, Mary Tool, Pittstere, Pennsylvania and Nellie Donovan of Los Angeles, California were listed in her will. James B. Greene was the administrator of her estate.

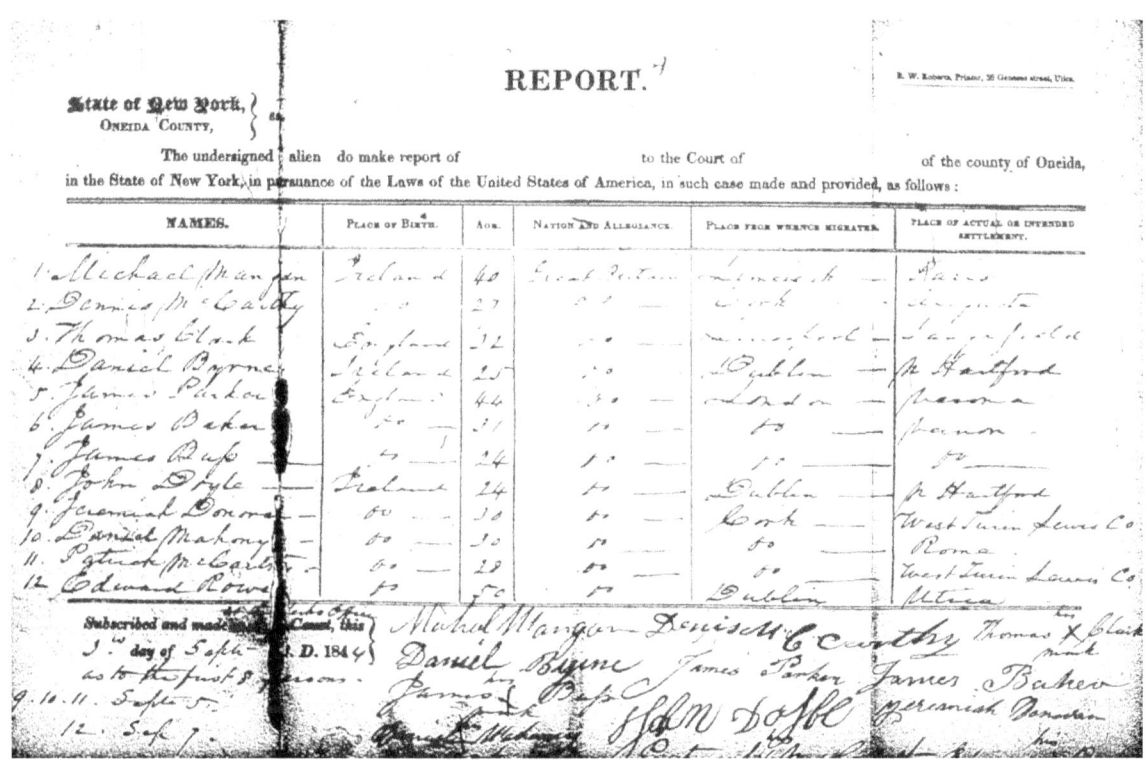

Declaration of intent report from Oneida County, New York, of Jeremiah Donovan indicating he was born Ireland, 30 years old, came from County Cork Ireland and was going to West Turin, Lewis County, New York.

---

[9] 1850 Annsville, New York Census

[10] 1850 Annsville, New York Census

[11] Obituary, Utica Newspaper, March 21, 1925

[12] Tombstone, St. Mary's Cemetery, Florence, New York

[13] Tombstone, St. Mary's Cemetery, Florence, New York

4.   vi.   Dennis C. Donovan was born in 1850 in Oneida County, New York[14] and died in 1892[15].

5.   vii.   Jeremiah Donovan Jr was born April 07, 1850 in Florence, New York[16] and died June 03, 1917 in Florence, New York[17].

      viii.   Michael Donovan was born in 1853 in New York State[18].   Michael was not listed with his family in the 1870 Osceola, New York Census. He was also not alive in 1909 when his sister, Catherine, died.

Generation Two

2. Mary Ann Donovan[2] (Jeremiah Donovan[1]) was born in October 1836 in Amsterdam, New York[19] and died on December 12, 1911 in St. Elizabeth Hospital, Utica, New York[20]. She married John H. Clancy in 1855[21]. He was born on April 22, 1834 in Ireland[22] and died on July 30, 1914 in St. Elizabeth Hospital, Utica, New York[23]. Mary Ann died of Diabetes and had been ill for 2 years prior to her death. She was able to read and write. She was a member of St. Patrick's Church and the Sacred Heart Society. She came to Utica 25 years prior to her death. They lived in New York Mills, New York in 1888 and later moved to Utica, New York. For more on Mary Ann Donovan and John H. Clancy, see Chapter Three.

3. Margaret Donovan[2] (Jeremiah Donovan[1]) was born in 1843 in New York State and died on March 20, 1925 in Utica, New York[24]. She married George McEvoy before 1875. He was born in 1814[25] and died on September 22, 1884 in Utica, New York[26]. She was married to a man by the name of Kiley in 1888 at the time of her father's death. The 1889 Utica Directory listed Margaret Kiley as a widow living at 93 Steuben St., Utica, New York. She later married William H. Hill in 1893[27], the son of Alderman

---

[14] Tombstone, St. Mary's Cemetery, Florence, New York

[15] Tombstone, St. Mary's Cemetery, Florence, New York

[16] Family Information from Kevin Miller

[17] New York State Vital Records

[18] 1860 Osceola, New York Census

[19] Obituary, Utica Newspaper December 13, 1911

[20] Obituary, Utica Newspaper December 13, 1911

[21] 1900 Utica, New York Census, Ward 11

[22] Death Certificate

[23] Death Certificate

[24] Obituary, Utica Newspaper, March 21, 1925

[25] Death Announcement, Utica Newspaper September 23, 1884

[26] Death Announcement, Utica Newspaper September 23, 1884

[27] 1910 Utica, New York Census

Luke Hill. He was born on August 02, 1856 in Utica, New York[28] and died on April 20, 1930 in Utica, New York[29].

Margaret was baptized September 3, 1843 in St. Peter's Church, Rome, New York. The sponsors were Patrick McCarthy and Johana Hallahn. Margaret had had pneumonia for ten days prior to her death. Margaret was a member of St. Francis deSales Church. She had spent the greater part of her life in Utica.

William H. Hill was educated in Assumption Academy and as a young man worked with his father. He was in the wholesale liquor business in this city for 37 years and a member of the firm of Donahue, Riedel & Hill, 10 Lafayette Street, Utica, New York. He was a member of St. Francis deSales Church.

Children of Margaret Donovan and George McEvoy are:
1.   i.   Mary M. McEvoy was born in 1875 in New York State[30] and died January 26, 1954 in Utica, New York[31].
        ii.   Catherine F. McEvoy was born in 1875 in Utica, New York[32] and died January 08, 1931 in Utica, New York[33].   Catherine's body was found in West Utica after she had a heart attack in front of 1308 West Street. She was rushed to Faxton Hospital, but was unable to be saved. She was in the hospital for more than 12 hours before she was identified. Catherine lived with her mother and William Hill in the 1910 and 1920 Utica Census. She was a member of St. Francis deSales Church. She was educated in Utica and lived there all her life.

4. Dennis C. Donovan[2] (Jeremiah Donovan[1]) was born in 1850 in Oneida County, New York[34] and died in 1892[35]. He married a girl by the name of Elizabeth about 1871. She was born in 1853 in New York State[36] and died in 1911[37].   In the 1880 Florence, New York Census listed Elizabeth as the head of the family.

Dennis C. Donovan and Elizabeth had the following children:
        i.   Mary A. Donovan was born in 1872 in New York State[38].
        ii.   Francis Donovan was born in 1873 in New York State[39].

---

[28] Obituary, Utica Newspaper, April 20, 1930
[29] Obituary, Utica Newspaper, April 20, 1930
[30] 1920 Rome, New York, Census
[31] Obituary, Utica Newspaper, January 27, 1954
[32] Obituary, Utica Newspaper, January 9, 1931
[33] Obituary, Utica Newspaper, January 9, 1931
[34] Tombstone, St. Mary's Cemetery, Florence, New York
[35] Tombstone, St. Mary's Cemetery, Florence, New York
[36] 1880 Florence, New York Census
[37] Tombstone, St. Mary's Cemetery, Florence, New York
[38] 1880 Florence, New York Census
[39] 1880 Florence, New York Census

iii.   John Donovan was born in 1875[40].
iv.   Dennis W. Donovan was born in 1877[41] and died in 1892[42].
v.   Charles Donovan was born in 1879[43].

5. Jeremiah Donovan Jr.[2] (Jeremiah Donovan[1]) was born on April 07, 1850 in Florence, New York[44] and died on June 03, 1917 in Florence, New York[45]. He married Elizabeth Ann McGovern about 1885 in Camden, New York[46], the daughter of Francis and Eleanor McGovern. She was born on August 13, 1857 in the Town of Camden, New York[47] and died on February 12, 1927 at 1605 Sunset Avenue, Utica, New York[48].   Jerry lived in Osceola, New York in 1911. Jerry's estate totaled $3012.50 with expenses of $200. On March 4, 1895, Jeremiah was running on the Republican ticket for supervisor of Osceola, New York. In 1908 Jeremiah was the assessor of Osceola.

The Camden Advance Journal - Florence - Thursday, May 12, 1927.
The body of Elizabeth Donovan who died in Utica last winter will be interred in St. Mary's Cemetery.

Jeremiah Donovan Jr and Elizabeth Ann McGovern had the following children:
2.   i.   Francis John Donovan was born August 29, 1886 in Florence, New York[49] and died October 07, 1964 in Utica, New York[50].

Photo of Francis John Donovan from the collection of Jerome Donovan and used with permission.

[40] 1880 Florence, New York Census
[41] Tombstone, St. Mary's Cemetery, Florence, New York
[42] Tombstone, St. Mary's Cemetery, Florence, New York
[43] 1880 Florence, New York Census
[44] Family information form Kevin Miller
[45] New York State Vital Records
[46] Obituary Utica Newspaper, February 12, 1927
[47] Obituary Utica Newspaper, February 12, 1927
[48] Obituary Utica Newspaper, February 12, 1927
[49] Family information form Kevin Miller
[50] Obituary Utica Newspaper, October 8, 1964

3.   ii.   Leo George Donovan was born January 16, 1887 in Osceola, New York[51], and died August 09, 1945 in Memorial Hospital, Utica, New York[52].

iii.   Loretta F. Donovan was born May 28, 1890 in New York State[53] and died December 1934[54]. She married James R. McNamara on March 03, 1919 in St. Patrick's Church, Utica, New York[55]. Loretta lived in Minneapolis, Minnesota, in 1921 and 1927. The 1930 Minneapolis Census did not mention any children.   A funeral announcement in the Utica Observer Dispatch Dec 31, 1934 said Loretta was buried in St. Mary's Cemetery in Florence, New York. I am not sure of her place of death or exact date.

iv.   Mabel Veronica Donovan was born in 1893 in Osceola, New York[56] and died April 22, 1921 at 1505 Sunset Ave., Utica, New York[57]. Mabel died ten days after she came down with Typhoid Fever. She spent her girlhood days in Florence, New York and came to Utica several years later. She was a graduate of the public schools of Camden and in 1912 of the training school connected with the Clinton High School. In her work of teaching in several of the smaller towns about the city, the largest of which was the school at Hart's Hill, Whitestown, she was very successful. She was a member of the St. Patrick's Church, Utica, New York.

4.   v.   Alice Irene Donovan was born April 13, 1897 in New York State[58] and died February 22, 1978 in St. Luke's Memorial Hospital, New Hartford, New York[59].

vi.   Ellen (Eleanor) Catherine Donovan was born October 31, 1899 in New York State and died January 27, 1902 in Osceola, New York[60].

Generation Three

1. Mary M. McEvoy[3] (Margaret Donovan[2], Jeremiah Donovan[1]) was born in 1875 in New York State[61] and died on January 26, 1954 in Utica, New York[62]. She married William Peter Claesgens on June 19, 1895 in St. Francis deSales Church, Utica, New York[63], the son of Col. Peter Claesgens and Mary Nightingale. He was born in 1870 in New York State[64] and died on June 21, 1921 in 12 Johnson Park, Utica, New York[65].

---

[51] Obituary Utica Newspaper, August 10, 1945
[52] Obituary Utica Newspaper, August 10, 1945
[53] Family information form Kevin Miller
[54] Funeral Announcement, Utica Newspaper, December 31, 1934
[55] Wedding Announcement, Utica Newspaper
[56] Obituary Utica Newspaper, April 23, 1921
[57] Obituary Utica Newspaper, April 23, 1921
[58] Obituary Utica Newspaper, February 23, 1978
[59] Obituary Utica Newspaper, February 23, 1978
[60] Family information form Kevin Miller
[61] 1920 Rome, New York, Census
[62] Obituary Utica Newspaper, January 27, 1954
[63] Marriage Announcement, Utica Newspaper, June 20, 1895
[64] 1920 Rome, New York, Census
[65] Obituary, Utica Newspaper, June 22, 1921

Mary was educated in Utica Schools. She was a communicant of St. Francis deSales Church. William lived his entire life in Utica, NY. He had been employed by the Utica Uniform Company. He was also a member of St. Francis de Sales Church and the Royal Arcanum.

Mary M. McEvoy and William Peter Claesgens had the following children:

   i.   George Edward Claesgens was born April 28, 1896 in New York State[66] and died March 02, 1983 in Livermore, Alameda, California[67]. George married a girl by the name of Loretta and they had one son who may still be living.

   ii.   Agnes M. Claesgens was born on August 14, 1902 in New York State[68] and died June 11, 2000 in St. Elizabeth Medical Center, Utica, NY[69]. Agnes graduated from St. Francis de Sales School. She was a nurse's aide employed by the Masonic Home, Faxton Hospital and also worked as private duty.

2. Francis John Donovan[3] (Jeremiah Donovan Jr.[2], Jeremiah Donovan[1]) was born on August 29, 1886 in Florence, New York[70] and died on October 07, 1964 in Utica, New York[71]. He married Evelyna Rose Hurley on July 14, 1919 in St. John's Church, Utica, New York[72], the daughter of Cornelius Hurley and Rose Kilkenny. She was born on March 14, 1891 in Remsen, New York[73] and died on March 20, 1983 in St. Joseph's Nursing Home, Utica, New York[74].

Photo of the children of Francis John Donovan. Back row left to right: James Hubert, Marjorie Frances, and Joseph Francis. Front row left to right: Shirley Mae, Mable Evelyn, and Cecelia Marilyn from the collection of Karen Donovan and used with permission.

---

[66] California Death Index
[67] California Death Index
[68] Social Security Death Index at Ancestry.com
[69] Social Security Death Index at Ancestry.com
[70] Family information form Kevin Miller
[71] Obituary Utica Newspaper, October 8, 1964
[72] Wedding Announcement, Utica Newspaper
[73] Obituary Utica Newspaper, March 21, 1983
[74] Obituary Utica Newspaper, March 21, 1983

Francis graduated from Albany Business College and taught school for a few years in Florence, New York. He then was employed by the United States Express Agency in New York City. After his marriage in 1918, he lived in Holland Patent, New York, and operated a farm for 15 years. In 1933 he returned to Utica where he was a steel worker for various local companies. He retired in 1959. He was a member of Sacred Heart Church, its Holy Name Society and the Iron Workers Union. Lena was born in Remsen, New York and moved to Utica in her early childhood. She and her husband operated a dairy farm in the Town of Marcy. She returned to Utica in 1934 and was a member of Sacred Heart Church and the Whitestown Senior Citizens.

Photo of Joseph Francis and James Hubert Donovan with their mother, Evelyna Rose Hurley Donovan from the collection of Karen Donovan and used with permission.

Francis John Donovan and Evelyna Rose Hurley had the following children:

    6.   i.   Marjorie Frances Donovan was born August 18, 1920 and died May 27, 2000[75].

    7.   ii.   Joseph Francis Donovan was born February 08, 1922 in Utica, New York[76] and died August 26, 1988 in Utica, New York[77].

    8.   iii.   James Hubert Donovan was born November 12, 1923 in Marcy, New York and died August 31, 1990 in Chadwicks, New York[78].

Baby photo of James Hubert Donovan from the collection of Karen Donovan and used with permission.

9.   iv.   Mabel Evelyn Donovan was born October 24, 1925 in Holland Patent, New York[79], and died October 29, 2000 in St. Elizabeth Medical Center, Utica, New York[80].

     v.   Living Donovan

     vi.   Living Donovan

---

[75] Obituary Utica Newspaper, May 29, 2000
[76] Obituary Utica Newspaper, August 27, 1988
[77] Obituary Utica Newspaper, August 27, 1988
[78] Obituary Utica Newspaper, September 1, 1990
[79] Obituary Utica Newspaper, October 30, 2000
[80] Obituary Utica Newspaper, October 30, 2000

3. Leo George Donovan[3] (Jeremiah Donovan Jr.[2], Jeremiah Donovan[1]) was born on January 16, 1887 in Osceola, New York[81] and died on August 09, 1945 in Memorial Hospital, Utica, New York[82]. He married Frances Bridgette Salvey on April 22, 1918 in St. Vincent's Ferier Church, Yonkers, New York[83], the daughter of Daniel Salvey and Alice Dixon. She was born on December 05, 1884 in Camden, New York[84] and died on January 14, 1964 in New Hartford, New York[85].   Leo came to Utica in 1923 and had his own painting and carpentry business. He was member of St. Francis DeSales Church.

Leo George Donovan and Frances Bridgette Falvey had the following children:
10.   i.   Eleanor Mary Donovan was born April 22, 1919 in New York City, New York[86], and died April 02, 1999 in St. Luke's Home, New Hartford, New York[87].
11.   ii.   Daniel Leo Donovan was born June 11, 1920 in Utica, New York[88] and died March 05, 1981 in Utica, New York[89].
            iii.   Robert William Donovan was born August 20, 1921[90] and died April 09, 1978[91]. Robert lived in Penfield, New York, at the time of his death.   He served in Germany in World War II.   He worked for the Hallmark Company and more recently for the Standard Furniture Company in Herkimer, New York.
12.   iv.   John Edward Donovan was born October 31, 1922 in Utica, New York[92] and died May 06, 1962 in Binghamton, New York[93].

4. Alice Irene Donovan[3] (Jeremiah Donovan Jr.[2], Jeremiah Donovan[1]) was born on April 13, 1897 in New York State[94] and died on February 22, 1978 in St. Luke's Memorial Hospital, New Hartford, New York[95]. She married William Timothy McCarthy on September 20, 1932 in St. Patrick's Church, Utica, New York[96], the son of Jeremiah McCarthy and Johanna Erwin. He was born on May 24, 1886 in Florence, New York[97] and died on September 24, 1960 at 40 Clinton St., Whitesboro, New York[98].   Alice attended school in Florence and then attended the Excelsior Business School of Utica.

---

[81] Obituary Utica Newspaper, August 10, 1945
[82] Obituary Utica Newspaper, August 10, 1945
[83] Wedding Announcement, Utica Newspaper
[84] Family information form Kevin Miller
[85] Obituary Utica Newspaper, January 15, 1964
[86] Obituary Utica Newspaper, April 3, 1999
[87] Obituary Utica Newspaper of husband, Warren Johnson, June 13, 1985
[88] Obituary Utica Newspaper, March 6, 1981
[89] Obituary Utica Newspaper, March 6, 1981
[90] Social Security Death Index at Ancestry.com
[91] Obituary Utica Newspaper, April 11, 1978
[92] Obituary Utica Newspaper, May 7, 1962
[93] Obituary Utica Newspaper, May 7, 1962
[94] Obituary Utica Newspaper, February 23, 1978
[95] Obituary Utica Newspaper, February 23, 1978
[96] Wedding Announcement, Utica Newspaper
[97] World War I draft registration on Ancestry.com
[98] Obituary Utica Newspaper, September 25, 1960

For many years she and her husband operated McCarthy's Restaurant in Whitesboro, New York. She was a member of St. Paul's Church in Whitesboro, New York. William attended school in Florence and Whitesboro. He was a member of St. Paul's Church and it's Holy Name Society.

Photo of Alice Irene Donovan and William Timothy McCarthy in their restaurant "McCarthy's" in Whitesboro, New York from the collection of Karen Donovan and used with permission.

Alice Irene Donovan and William Timothy McCarthy had the following children:

    i.   Living McCarthy

    ii.   James Edward McCarthy was born in 1934 in Utica, New York[99] and died December 01, 1975 in Utica, New York[100]. James was active in fast pitch softball leagues in the area. He was a pitcher and had played in the Northern League and McCarthy's A.C. League among others. He graduated from Whitesboro Central School in 1953. He was a member of St. Paul's Church and its Holy Name Society and the Liquor Dealers Association. He was the operator of McCarthy's Restaurant in Whitesboro.

Generation Four

6. Marjorie Frances Donovan[4] (Francis John Donovan[3], Jeremiah Donovan Jr.[2], Jeremiah Donovan[1]) was born August 18, 1920 in Utica, New York and died May 27, 2000 at St. Luke's Memorial Hospital Center, New Hartford, New York[101]. Marjorie married Harold Kofpku, Joseph M. Herman, Robert Owen and James Arthur Prichard. Marjorie graduated from Whitesboro High School. She was a member of St. Paul's Church in Whitesboro, New York and its Women's Club. She served on the Oneida County Board of Elections, was past President of the Whitestown Republican Club, and a member of the New Hartford American Legion Post #1376 Auxiliary, the Whitestown senior citizens, the Oneida County Women's Republican Club and the AARP. She volunteered for Hospice Care, Inc. the Stanley Theatre League, Munson Williams Proctor Institute, Monday Night Downtown, Oneida County visitor's Bureau, Office of the aged and the Utica Boilermaker. She was honored as the 1995 Oneida County Senior citizen of the Year. Marge will be remembered as the Ultimate Volunteer and will be missed by many. She took great pride in her Irish heritage. Marjorie had three children who may still be living.

---

[99] Obituary Utica Newspaper, December 2, 1975
[100] Obituary Utica Newspaper, December 2, 1975
[101] Obituary Utica Newspaper, May 29, 2000

7. Joseph Francis Donovan[4] (Francis John Donovan[3], Jeremiah Donovan Jr.[2], Jeremiah Donovan[1]) was born on February 08, 1922 in Utica, New York[102] and died on August 26, 1988 in Utica, New York[103]. He was married on February 09, 1946 in Blessed Sacrament Church, Utica, New York[104]. Joseph was employed at Griffiss Air Force Base. During that time he received a special Air Force Commendation for outstanding service in the face of possible disaster. He was a World War II Army Veteran having served in the European Theater and was an active participant in the D-Day Invasion. He was a Catholic. Joseph Francis Donovan and his wife had three children who may still be living.

Photo of Joseph Francis Donovan from the collection of Karen Donovan and used with permission.

8. James Hubert Donovan[4] (Francis John Donovan[3], Jeremiah Donovan Jr.[2], Jeremiah Donovan[1]) was born on November 12, 1923 in Marcy, New York[105] and died on August 31, 1990 in Chadwicks, New York[106]. He married Esther Roselle Moretti on September 27, 1947 at St. Anthony of Padua Church, Chadwicks, New York[107], the daughter of Anthony Moretti and Lebra Delmedico. She was born on April 26, 1922 in Utica, New York[108] and died on December 09, 2007 in St. Joseph's Nursing Home, Utica, New York[109]. James graduated from Whitesboro High School and served in the United States Marine Corps in World War II. He moved to Chadwicks after his marriage and was a member of St. Anthony of Padua Church in Chadwicks, New York. He was elected as Councilman, Town of New Hartford, New York, in 1961 and Supervisor of the Town of New Hartford in 1964. He was elected New York State Senator in 1965 and served for 25 years. He received a degree in Honorary Doctorate of law in May 1990 in Wadhams Hall Seminary College Ogdensburg, New York.

Photo of James Hubert Donovan from the collection of Karen Donovan and used with permission.

---

[102] Obituary Utica Newspaper, August 26, 1988
[103] Obituary Utica Newspaper, August 26, 1988
[104] Wedding Announcement, Utica Newspaper
[105] Obituary Utica Newspaper, September 1, 1990
[106] Obituary Utica Newspaper, September 1, 1990
[107] Obituary Utica Newspaper, December 10, 2007
[108] Obituary Utica Newspaper, December 10, 2007
[109] Obituary Utica Newspaper, December 10, 2007

Esther was raised and educated in Chadwicks, New York and worked at the Rome Air Depot, the Utica Bleachery Company and the Standard Silk Mill Company, both in Chadwicks, New York. She was a member of St. Anthony of Padua Church and its Altar Rosary Society, the Republican 100,000 Club and the Women's Republican Club of Utica. She was a member of the Edward L. Clonan American Legion Post 1000 Ladies Auxiliary. James Hubert Donovan and Esther Roselle Moretti had seven children who may still be living.

9. Mabel Evelyn Donovan[4] (Francis John Donovan[3],Jeremiah Donovan Jr.[2], Jeremiah Donovan[1]) was born on October 24, 1925 in Holland Patent, New York[110]and died on October 29, 2000 in St. Elizabeth Medical Center, Utica, New York[111]. She married Donald Arthur Irion on May 14, 1949 in Sacred Heart Church, Utica, New York[112], the son of Irving Irion and Florence Morrow. He was born on August 04, 1925 in Utica, New York[113] and died on February 20, 1994 in St. Elizabeth Hospital, Utica, New York[114]. Mabel worked for her brother, the late Senator James H. Donovan, both in his private business and while he served as New York State Senator. She later was employed with the St. John the Evangelist Church, New Hartford, New York and its school, and was a member of St. John the Evangelist Church. Donald attended Utica Schools and worked for Chicago Pneumatic for 33 years. He was a member of St. John the Evangelist Church in New Hartford, New York. Mabel Evelyn Donovan and Donald Arthur Irion had two children who may still be living.

10. Eleanor Mary Donovan[4] (Leo George Donovan[3], Jeremiah Donovan Jr.[2], Jeremiah Donovan[1]) was born on April 22, 1919 in New York City, New York[115] and died on April 02, 1999 in St. Luke's Home, New Hartford, New York[116]. She married Warren Woodruff Johnson on May 01, 1942 in Columbus, Georgia, the son of Warren Johnson and Florence Zippler. He was born on March 30, 1917 in Pleasantville, New Jersey[117] and died on June 12, 1985 in Utica, New York[118]. Eleanor graduated from St. Francis deSales High School and later attended Mohawk Valley Community College. For many years, until her retirement in 1991, she was employed by the Oneida County Department of Social Services as a legal secretary. Eleanor was a member of Historic Old St. John's Church, Utica, New York where she was a Lay Minister. She was also a member of the Women's Club of the church and was an associate member of the Sisters of St. Joseph of Carondolet. She was also a member of the CSJ Associates.

---

[110] Obituary Utica Newspaper, October 30, 2000
[111] Obituary Utica Newspaper, October 30, 2000
[112] Wedding Announcement, Utica Newspaper
[113] Obituary Utica Newspaper, February 21, 1994
[114] Obituary Utica Newspaper, February 21, 1994
[115] Obituary Utica Newspaper, April 3, 1999
[116] Obituary Utica Newspaper, April 3, 1999
[117] Obituary Utica Newspaper, June 13, 1985
[118] Obituary Utica Newspaper, June 13, 1985

Warren was educated in Pleasantville and Atlantic City, New Jersey. He attended the Drexel University in Pennsylvania. He was a veteran of the United States Army serving in the South Pacific Theater in World War II. He was employed by Kelsey Hayes until his retirement in 1983. He was a member of Old Historic St. Johns Church, Utica, New York.

Eleanor Mary Donovan and Warren Woodruff Johnson had the following children:

    i.   Maureen Anne Johnson was born February 03, 1945[119] and died August 06, 1951[120].

    ii.   Living Johnson
    iii.   Living Johnson
    iv.   Living Johnson
    v.   Living Johnson
    vi.   Living Johnson
    vii.   Living Johnson

11. Daniel Leo Donovan[4] (Leo George Donovan[3], Jeremiah Donovan Jr.[2], Jeremiah Donovan[1]) was born on June 11, 1920 in Utica, New York[121] and died on March 05, 1981 in Utica, New York[122]. He married Marie Eva Juliette Cordeau on May 22, 1948, the daughter of Robert Cordeau and Marie Arcand. She was born on October 06, 1921 in Biddeford, Maine[123] and died on December 09, 1980 in Utica, New York[124]. For many years Daniel was the purchasing agent for the Utica Knitting Company and in later years he was the co-owner of the All Make Typewriter Company in Whitesboro, New York. He was a member of St. John's Evangelist Church in New Hartford, New York and had served in the United States Navy during World War II. Juliette's early education was in parochial schools in Biddeford, Maine. She came to Utica as a young woman and graduated from St. Frances deSales High School in 1941. She married George Stone who was killed during World War II. She was a customer service representative at the Savings Bank of Utica, New Hartford Branch, and a member of St. Johns Evangelist Church in New Hartford, New York. Daniel Leo Donovan and Marie Eva Juliette Cordeau had two children who may still be living.

---

[119] Family information form Kevin Miller
[120] Family information form Kevin Miller
[121] Obituary Utica Newspaper, March 6, 1981
[122] Obituary Utica Newspaper, March 6, 1981
[123] Obituary Utica Newspaper, December 10, 1980
[124] Obituary Utica Newspaper, December 10, 1980

12. John Edward Donovan[4] (Leo George Donovan[3], Jeremiah Donovan Jr.[2], Jeremiah Donovan[1]) was born on October 31, 1922 in Utica, New York[125] and died on May 06, 1962 in Binghamton, New York[126]. John served in Lido Beach, Long Island, in World War II with the United States Navy. He had lived in Vestal for ten years and was employed as an automobile salesman. He was a graduate of St. Francis de Sales Grammar and High School. He was a member of Our Lady of Sorrows Church, Vestal, New York. John Edward Donovan and his wife had four children who may still be living.

[125] Obituary Utica Newspaper, May 7, 1962
[126] Obituary Utica Newspaper, May 7, 1962

Index

The index lists all people mentioned in the book. Women are listed under their maiden names and married names. Women's maiden names are in ( ); their married names are in [ ]. Nicknames are denoted with { }.

Individuals with unknown surnames are listed at the beginning of the index.